Student Study Guide

Volume II

for use with

Books 4–6 and Volume II
of the Two-Volume Edition

The Humanistic Tradition

Fourth Edition

Gloria K. Fiero

McGraw Hill

Boston   Burr Ridge, IL   Dubuque, IA   Madison, WI   New York
San Francisco   St. Louis   Bangkok   Bogotá   Caracas   Kuala Lumpur
Lisbon   London   Madrid   Mexico City   Milan   Montreal   New Delhi
Santiago   Seoul   Singapore   Sydney   Taipei   Toronto

McGraw-Hill Higher Education

A Division of The **McGraw-Hill** Companies

Student Study Guide Volume II for use with Books 4–6 and Volume II of the Two-Volume Edition
THE HUMANISTIC TRADITION

1234567890BKM/BKM0987654321

ISBN 0-07-238849-8

www.mhhe.com

TABLE OF CONTENTS

This Study Guide is designed to provide you with a variety of methods for learning the materials presented in *The Humanistic Tradition,* Fourth Edition, by Gloria K. Fiero. It should be used along with *The Humanistic Tradition* and follows closely the format of Chapters 20 through 38 in Volume II of the two-volume edition and Books 4, 5, and 6 of the minibook edition. The Study Guide will assist you in understanding the major ideas and themes in the global humanities. It should also help you to master those terms and concepts on which you may be tested. The perforated pages in this guide allow you to tear out and submit various exercises if assigned by your instructor.

FORMAT OF THE STUDY GUIDE

Each chapter in the Study Guide is divided into sections, the contents of which are explained below:

I. CHAPTER OBJECTIVE

The Chapter Objective describes the main topic or thesis of the chapter. It is followed by a section (AM I FAMILIAR WITH?) that prompts you to summarize the most important ideas and themes in the chapter.

II. OUTLINE

The Outline provides a brief overview of the chapter. The Outline is like a roadmap that tells you where you are going and which "landmarks" you will encounter on the way.

III. KEY TERMS

After reading the chapter in the textbook, you should review the terms in this list. Try to **define each** of the Key Terms, explaining in your own words what each term means and how or why it is important to the theme of the chapter. If you cannot recall the term, return to the relevant page in the textbook or to the chapter glossary in which it may be listed. A pronunciation guide is provided for those terms that might be difficult to pronounce. (PRONUNCIATION KEY appears at the end of the introduction.)

IV. KEY NAMES

After reading the chapter in the textbook, you should be able to identify the persons, places, or titles in this list. Pretend you have been stopped by visitors from the planet Mars: they ask you <u>who</u> Leonardo da Vinci was—that is, <u>what</u> he did and <u>why</u> Earthlings still admire him—<u>when</u> he lived (approximately), and <u>where</u> he lived. If you cannot make a complete identification, go back to the textbook. The more precise you make your identification, the better you will be able to illustrate your general themes and ideas in classroom discussion and writing exercises. As with the Key Terms, a pronunciation guide is provided to assist you with names you might find difficult to pronounce.

V. KEY DATES

Key dates are provided as chronological signposts for review. These dates should assist you in establishing historical continuity; they are not intended as additional information for memorization. To help you relate world events to the arts, study the Time Lines that are provided throughout the textbook.

VI. VOCABULARY BUILDING

The words in this section are taken from each chapter. They may or may not be familiar to you, depending on the size of your vocabulary. If, after reading the chapter, you find that you cannot define one of the words on this list, look it up in any standard dictionary; then give the meaning in your own words. By doing so, you will work to increase your vocabulary.

VII. SAMPLE MULTIPLE CHOICE QUESTIONS

After you have finished studying the chapter, test yourself by answering the Sample Multiple Choice Questions in this section. The correct answers appear on the last page of this Introduction. If you have answered any question incorrectly, return to the textbook to review the pertinent material.

VIII. VISUAL/SPATIAL EXERCISE

This type of exercise will appear in most, but not all, chapters. You may be asked to locate and label geographic place names on maps that are provided in the Study Guide. Other Visual Exercises challenge you to identify the structural or decorative parts of a building for which architectural floor plans and elevations (similar to those that appear in the textbook) are provided.

Finally, for some chapters in thus Guide, there are geometric diagrams (see page 3) labeled with key words and phrases. These "graphic clusters"* prompt you to make free and intuitive connections and associations between events, terms, and concepts. You may write within or across the geometric shapes, make notes concerning each movement or style, use arrows to show directions of influence, related ideas, and so on. Graphic clusters, like the "windows" of a computer screen, provide an alternative to linear modes of organizing data.

IX. ESSAY QUESTIONS

The Essay Questions for each chapter are designed to help you think creatively about the materials presented in the chapter. You may wish to read the essay questions before you read the chapter in your textbook and return to them for review prior to exams.

X. MAKING CONNECTIONS

This exercise challenges you to relate the materials you have studied to your own personal life experience. You may use these ideas for class discussion or for writing exercises—or simply to stimulate creative thinking. There are no "wrong" answers.

XI. SYNTHESIS

At the end of each Part division, you will find questions that ask you to synthesize (or bring together into a larger whole) a group of related ideas and themes presented in that Part of the textbook. These questions are useful for reviewing large blocks of material prior to mid-term and final exams.

XII. BONUS

The Bonus pages in the Study Guide supply visual diagrams and information that enlarge upon the contents of a chapter.

HOW TO READ THE TEXTBOOK

You may read your textbook for sheer entertainment, but as a student, it is likely that you will also need to read in order to prepare for exams on the contents of the text. Here are some tips on how to read the textbook with an eye toward remembering what you read:

Read attentively. If you are not reading in a favorable environment, you will remember little of what you read. To check on whether you are reading attentively, put down your book every fifteen minutes and ask yourself what you have just read. If you cannot summarize what you have learned, begin again, or wait until conditions permit you to read attentively.

*Adapted from Gabriele L. Rico, *Writing the Natural Way* (N.Y.: St. Martin's Press, 1983).

1. Read the <u>chapter title</u> carefully before you begin the body of the chapter. What is the main subject and the focus of this chapter? As you read, you should be attentive to the boldfaced key headings that appear throughout the chapter; they are like signposts on a highway: they give direction to the content of the chapter.

2. Read the <u>summary</u> at the end of the chapter before AND after you read the body of the chapter. The summary brings together the major themes and ideas discussed in the chapter.

3. Read <u>actively</u>. To increase your attention to the material, read with pen or pencil in hand and underline or highlight key words, phrases, and sentences. Make marginal notes that summarize *in your own words* the main ideas in the passage you have read. The underlined words and marginal notes will help you to recall the content when you review the material prior to exams. Writing marginal notes has great value: studies show that students remember better what they write than what they read or hear. Another active study technique involves taking notes on what you are reading, or creating your own outline of the material. Try using the Chapter Outline provided in the Study Guide as a framework for such notes.

4. Look slowly and carefully at each of the <u>visual illustrations</u> in the textbook. As you read through a chapter, allot time to analyze each of the illustrations (Figures, Maps, Line Drawings, etc.). Be sure to read the captions beneath the photographs and the keys to the maps. The illustrations of original paintings and sculptures in your textbook are valuable primary sources: think of them as your world tour through the arts.

5. Read the <u>poetry</u> in these chapters aloud. Many of your Readings are complete poems or excerpts from longer poetic works. Most poems were intended to be spoken rather than read and are best appreciated (and remembered) when heard.

6. Make active use of the study aids provided in the textbook. After reading the chapter, review the items listed in the *Glossary* to each chapter. Before exams, check the *Time Lines* that appear at the beginning of each Part division for an overview of the chronology of world events, literature, visual arts, and music. If you wish to read further, or if your instructor invites extra credit reports, choose a book from the *Suggestions for Reading* at the end of each chapter.

7. Make <u>connections</u>. Look for thematic and stylistic connections between the parts of the chapters and between the chapters in each Book. Seek connections also to your own personal experiences, especially those gained by engaging the arts firsthand. *The Humanistic Tradition* provides you with many exciting masterworks, the finest available in print and image; but there is no substitute for engaging the arts <u>directly</u>, that is, for viewing original paintings and sculptures in museums and galleries, for hearing music performed in concert halls, and for seeing staged and/or filmed productions of theatrical works and dance performances.

TIPS FOR STUDYING THE GLOBAL HUMANITIES

The textbook consists of PRIMARY sources and SECONDARY information. Primary sources are works that are original to the age in which they were produced. The primary source may be a drawing, a painting, or a piece of music. The secondary information is the author's assessment of the material. It offers interpretation and analysis. Some students feel swamped by the large amount of materials that is presented in humanities survey courses. A method that has proved helpful in managing the content of the course is to approach each of the primary sources from the triple vantage point of TEXT, CONTEXT, and SUBTEXT.

THE TEXT: The <u>text</u> is the BODY OR SUBSTANCE OF THE PRIMARY SOURCE. Ask yourself about the text:

1. What is its MEDIUM, that is, what is it made of? Is it made of clay, stone, a group of words, sounds in rhythmic progression?

2. What is its FORM? That is, what is its specific or outward shape? Is it a wall painting, a free-standing sculpture? a poem? a chant? (The section below on THE FORMAL ELEMENTS OF THE ARTS will help you refine your understanding in this area.)

3. What is its CONTENT? that is, what subject matter or message (if any) does it mean to relate?

THE CONTEXT: The context refers to the HISTORICAL AND CULTURAL MILIEU in which the text was produced. Ask yourself about the context of the primary source: In what time and place did the text originate? How did it function in its own time? Did it serve the religious needs of the community? the political needs? purely aesthetic needs?

SUBTEXT: The subtext refers to the SECONDARY OR IMPLIED MEANINGS of the primary source: What does the text imply? What do the implications suggest about the age in which the text was created? Is the implied meaning religious? political? Does the subtext have an affective (emotion-stirring) charge?

You will discover that by organizing your study of the primary sources around these central concepts, your mastery of the material will be greatly enhanced, in part, because your analysis of the text, context, and subtext will engage you in the process of critical thinking about THE HUMANISTIC TRADITION.

THE FORMAL ELEMENTS OF THE ARTS

Each of the arts reflects an aspect of our daily lives: as creatures of language, we speak and read the words that comprise LITERATURE; we see the shapes and images that constitute THE VISUAL ARTS; we live and work in the structures that belong to the world of ARCHITECTURE; we hear the sounds in time that constitute MUSIC; and move through space with the gestures of the DANCE.

Artists organize these elements in ways that turn words into poems, colors into images, and sounds into music. The key to understanding and enjoying the arts is ENGAGEMENT, that is, the willful investment of time and thoughtful attention. Each of the arts requires a slightly different kind of engagement, and each rewards the participant in a different way.

When we first encounter a work of literature, art, or music, we may know little about how or where the text originated; yet, we may experience a strong affective response. However, our engagement with the text will be greatly enhanced by the critical facilities we bring to it. The more we know about the formal elements of the text, the richer our experience is likely to be. The terms presented below should help you heighten your critical attention and refine your engagement with each of the arts.

THE LITERARY ARTS

PROSE AND POETRY: Every literary work, whether it is intended to be spoken aloud or read silently, employs the medium of language, but literary FORM varies according to the manner in which words are arranged. So POETRY, which shares with music and dance the virtue of RHYTHMIC ORGANIZATION, may be distinguished from PROSE, which normally lacks regular, rhythmic, organizational patterns. The main purpose of prose is to narrate, describe, or convey information, but also to evoke mood, feeling, and atmosphere. Histories, short stories, novels, and other narrative genres generally make use of prose. Poetry, a mode of expression that seeks to heighten affective response, often compresses language and takes liberties with conventional patterns of grammar. Poets employ a variety of literary devices (the names of which you will encounter throughout the text) in order to enhance the lyric or rhythmic qualities of the poem. These devices reflect the close association between poetry and music, both of which—because they are intended to be performed—may be thought of as PERFORMANCE arts (see below).

THE VISUAL ARTS

THE GRAPHIC ARTS: Painting, drawing, printmaking, and photography are two-dimensional (height/width), spatial art forms. These art forms generally make use of LINE and COLOR to produce various shapes and textures, the arrangement of which constitutes the DESIGN or COMPOSITION. In the graphic arts, SPACE is described by the contours of the line, the position of the shapes, and the intensity of the colors. Artists who seek to create the illusion of three-dimensionality on the flat (two-dimensional) surface or PICTURE PLANE use devices such as LINEAR PERSPECTIVE and AERIAL PERSPECTIVE. Artists also use a number of formal devices, such as TEXTURE and CONTRAST, to give expressive content to the visual object. Unlike words, the formal elements of line, color, and texture lack explicit meaning. Artists manipulate these formal elements to describe or interpret the visible world (as in such genres as portraiture and landscape); to create fantastic or imaginary images; and to explore the expressive qualities of the formal elements without regard to recognizable subject matter (thus producing nonrepresentational art).

SCULPTURE: Sculpture adds a third dimension, the dimension of depth, to the two dimensions of the graphic arts. The addition of depth increases the physical impact and presence of the artwork and invites the viewer to move around it in order to experience it fully. A sculpture may be executed in RELIEF, that is, as a carved surface that may be viewed only from the front and sides, or IN THE ROUND, that is, as a free-standing form. MASS and VOLUME work with SHAPE and TEXTURE to give sculpture its expressive content. A sculpture may be executed by means of the "subtractive" method of CARVING or CUTTING out of a substance (such as stone or wood), or by the "additive" methods of MODELING in soft materials (such as clay, wax, or plaster), which may be CAST in more permanent materials (such as bronze). Sculptures may also be ASSEMBLED or CONSTRUCTED from a variety of found or manufactured materials, including those of modern-day technology. KINETIC or "moving" sculpture, environmental "earthworks," and art that integrates spectacle and theatrical performance are modern forms of expression that deliberately blur distinctions among the arts.

ARCHITECTURE: Like sculpture, architecture is three-dimensional, but it is also expressly functional and normally large in scale. Architects enclose space to serve specific needs: domestic, communal, military, and religious. There is usually a close relationship between the FORM of an architectural structure and its FUNCTION, and between the DESIGN of a structure and its ENVIRONMENT. The architect uses a PLAN, or view of the interior spaces as seen from above the building or site; the ELEVATION is an architectural drawing that shows the front, rear, or side of a building as if it were sawed open to reveal an interior wall. In manipulating SPACE, architects are especially conscious of the relationships between SOLIDS and VOIDS, especially in their functional and symbolic potential.

THE PERFORMANCE ARTS

MUSIC: Music is the rhythmic organization of sounds in time. Like literature, music is durational: that is, it unfolds over the period of time in which it occurs, rather than all at once. Like drama and dance, music is a performance art: although individual sounds may be "read" as NOTES in written form known as a SCORE, music is incomplete without performance. The formal elements of music include RHYTHM (the movement of musical tones in time), MELODY (the patterning and phrasing of musical tones), HARMONY (the arrangement of different musical tones as sounded together), and TONE COLOR (the special qualities of tones as produced by voice or instrument). Like the formal elements that constitute visual arts, the formal elements of music lack symbolic content, but while the verbal and visual arts often describe or interpret, music is almost always nonrepresentational—it rarely "means" anything beyond sound itself. For that reason, music is the most difficult of the arts to describe in words and possibly the most powerful in affect.**

DRAMA: Drama is the most distinctly performance oriented of the verbal arts. Though a play may be read in a book or as a script, its expressive impact requires the unfolding of the language and the action in time and space. As THEATER, the staging of gesture and action complements the power of the spoken word. In live theater, as well as in the electronic media of film and television, dramatic performance often draws on or integrates aspects of all of the other arts.

OPERA: Opera is staged dramatic performance in which the characters sing (rather than speak), usually to instrumental accompaniment. Surely the most elaborate of the performance arts, opera integrates elements of the literary arts (such as drama), the visual arts (usually in the form of costumes and scenery), and dance, as well as music.

**Students may wish to purchase the Music Listening Compact Discs that accompany *The Humanistic Tradition* (available from McGraw-Hill Educational Services [1-800-338-3987] or your local bookstore). CD, Volume II contains twenty-six audio recordings of the music listening selections discussed in Chapters 20 to 38.

DANCE: Dance is an art form that uses the human body as a medium of expression. Like music, dance is durational: it unfolds in time. But like the visual arts, dance presents itself in space. A performance art, dance often integrates music and visual decor.

FILM: Film is a moving-image technology that draws on all of the other arts for its aesthetic impact. It is a durational medium that employs images and sounds that may or may not convey narrative and thematic content. Film (and other forms of video art) did not come into existence as a medium of expression until the early twentieth century; hence, it is treated only in chapters 32 to 38 of this textbook.

ONLINE LEARNING CENTER

A complete set of web-based resources for *The Humanistic Tradition* can be found at www.mhhe.com/fiero. Material for students includes study outlines, self-tests, interactive maps, timelines, additional bibliography, and links to other web resources.

ACKNOWLEDGMENTS

My thanks go to Darrell Bourque (University of Louisiana at Lafayette), James H. Dormon, and Laurinda Dixon (Syracuse University) for editorial suggestions related to the preparation of the Study Guide; to Risa P. Gorelick for assistance in producing the pronunciation guides, and to Chris Freitag, Nadia Bidwell, and Sarah Dermody (McGraw-Hill) for technical assistance.

PRONUNCIATION KEY

apple, play, ah (altar); egg, keep; inch, eye; glow, booze; outfit; bulk; u in book; single, shin, chapter, just; zebra, zhivago; canyon

ANSWERS TO THE SAMPLE MULTIPLE CHOICE QUESTIONS

Ch. 20: 1. c / 2. a / 3. b / 4. d / 5. b

Ch. 21: 1. d / 2. b / 3. a / 4. b / 5. b

Ch. 22: 1. b / 2. c / 3. a / 4. b / 5. b

Ch. 23: 1. c / 2. d / 3. a / 4. b / 5. b

Ch. 24: 1. c / 2. b / 3. d / 4. a / 5. b

Ch. 25: 1. b / 2. a / 3. d / 4. a / 5. c

Ch. 26: 1. b / 2. a / 3. c / 4. a / 5. d

Ch. 27: 1. d / 2. d / 3. a / 4. c / 5. b

Ch. 28: 1. c / 2. a / 3. b / 4. a / 5. d / 6. c

Ch. 29: 1. c / 2. a / 3. b / 4. a / 5. b

Ch. 30: 1. c / 2. b / 3. a / 4. d / 5. b / 6. d

Ch. 31: 1. b / 2. a / 3. c / 4. d / 5. b

Ch. 32: 1. b / 2. c / 3. a / 4. c / 5. c

Ch. 33: 1. a / 2. c / 3. c / 4. b / 5. a

Ch. 34: 1. c / 2. a / 3. b / 4. d / 5. c

Ch. 35: 1. c / 2. d / 3. b / 4. a / 5. c

Ch. 36: 1. c / 2. b / 3. b / 4. d / 5. d / 6. c

Ch. 37: 1. d / 2. c / 3. b / 4. a / 5. c / 6. d

Ch. 38: 1. a / 2. c / 3. b / 4. c / 5. d / 6. c

PART I: THE AGE OF THE BAROQUE

Chapter 20: The Catholic Reformation and the Baroque Style

I. CHAPTER OBJECTIVE:

To examine the impact of the Catholic Reformation (or Counter-Reformation) on the arts of the West

AM I FAMILIAR WITH:

- the spirit of Catholic reform as expressed in literature and art?
- the rise of mannerism and the baroque style?
- those features shared by baroque art and music?
- the significance of opera as a reflection of the baroque spirit?

II. OUTLINE

    A. Historical Context of the Catholic Reformation

        1. the Catholic Reformation in Europe

        2. Catholicism's reach into Asia and Latin America

    B. Catholic Reformation Mysticism

        1. Loyola and the Jesuit order

        2. visions of Saint Teresa

        3. religious ecstasy in the visual arts

    C. Rise of the Baroque Style

        1. roots in mannerism: El Greco

        2. baroque art: Bernini and Caravaggio

        3. Italian Baroque architecture

    D. Early Baroque Music

        1. sacred music: Palestrina

        2. polychoral composition: Gabrieli

        3. the birth of opera: Monteverdi

III. KEY TERMS: CAN I DEFINE/EXPLAIN?

(What? Why important?)

the "black virgin"

mannerism

trompe l'oeil [trahmp loy]

painterly

baroque

foreshortening

piazza [pee AHT zah]

baldacchino [bahl dah KEE now]

stucco

cartouche [kar TOOSH]

piano [PYAHN oh]

forte [FOR tay]

dynamics

tonality

chromatic scale

libretto

overture

aria [AHR ee ah]

recitative [re ci tah TIV]

pizzicato [pit si KAH tow]

opera

concertato [con cher TAH tow]

polychoral

IV. KEY NAMES: CAN I IDENTIFY?

(Who? What? When? Where?)

Loyola

Jesuits

Spiritual Exercises

Council of Trent

Guadalupe

Teresa of Avila [AH vee lah]

Crashaw

Michelangelo

Parmigianino [pahr me jyah NEE now]

Tintoretto [tin tow RET tow]

El Greco

Caravaggio [kar ah VAHJ yow]

Gentileschi [jen ti LES kee]

Apocrypha [ah POK re fah]

Bernini [ber NEE nee]

Pozzo [POT tsow]

da Vignola [dah VEE nyow lah]

Il Jesu [il HAY zoo]

Borromini [bow row MEE nee]

San Carlo alle Quattro Fontane [san KHAR low ahl KWART trow fown TAH nay]

Palestrina [pal I STREE nah]

Gabrieli [ga bree AY lee]

Saint Mark's Cathedral

Monteverdi [mahn te VER dee]

Orfeo [OR fey oh]

V. KEY DATES

- 1548 = Loyola publishes the *Spiritual Exercises*
- 1545-1563 = Council of Trent
- 1637 = first opera house built (Venice)

VI. VOCABULARY BUILDING: CAN I DEFINE?

dissident

impending

trapezoidal

ensemble

synthesis

VII. SAMPLE MULTIPLE CHOICE QUESTIONS

1. Dominikos Theotokopoulos, creator of *The Agony in the Garden,* is better known as

   a. Bernini.

   b. Tintoretto.

   c. El Greco.

   d. Caravaggio.

2. The style that most accurately describes Parmigianino's *Madonna of the Long Neck* is called

   a. mannerism.

   b. neoclassical.

   c. baroque.

   d. renaissance.

3. Characteristic of both Teresa's *Visions* and Bernini's *Ecstacy* is

   a. neoclassicism.

   b. sensuousness.

   c. rationalism.

   d. intricate detail.

4. Giovanni Gabrieli became celebrated for his

   a. expressive baroque paintings.

   b. design of Saint Mark's Cathedral.

   c. full-length operas.

   d. polychoral religious music.

5. The most spectacular feature of the Italian baroque church was the

   a. introduction of multiple naves.

   b. indulgence in illusionistic frescoes.

   c. revival of the early Renaissance facade.

   d. incorporation of fountains within the church.

(Answers appear on page x.)

VIII. VISUAL/SPATIAL EXERCISE

In the GRAPHIC CLUSTER on the next page, write freely to explore the relationships between the Catholic Reformation and the baroque style as configured in literature, the visual arts, and music. You may write within or across the "windows" in the cluster.

THE CATHOLIC REFORMATION AND THE BAROQUE STYLE

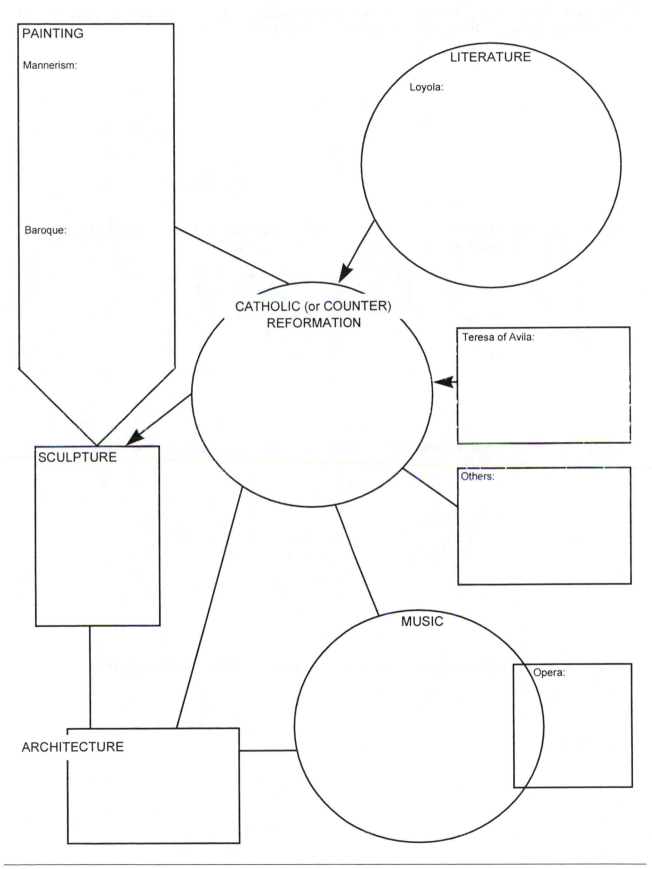

PAINTING

Mannerism:

Baroque:

LITERATURE

Loyola:

CATHOLIC (or COUNTER) REFORMATION

Teresa of Avila:

Others:

SCULPTURE

MUSIC

Opera:

ARCHITECTURE

IX. ESSAY QUESTIONS/WRITING EXERCISE

1. Describe the "theatrical effects" achieved by Bernini in his sculpture and architecture, by Caravaggio in painting, and by Gabrieli in music. In what ways do all of these works reflect the "baroque spirit"?

2. How do each of the following illustrate the ideals of the Catholic Reformation: Loyola's *Spiritual Exercises;* Bernini's *Ecstasy of Saint Teresa;* Pozzo's *Apotheosis of Saint Ignatius?*

3. Based on the primary sources (literary and visual) in this chapter, what roles might you assume women played in the early modern European world?

4. Discuss any single work found in this chapter from the perspective of text, context, and subtext.

X. MAKING CONNECTIONS

1. Describe a religious ritual or event that you have experienced firsthand. How did the physical setting (church, mosque, funeral home) affect your emotional response? In your answer, consider visual imagery, music, recitation of texts, and so on.

2. Attend the live performance of an opera (or musical drama); how did each aspect of the performance (drama, music, set, costumes, dance, etc.) contribute to the total effect?

3. Find a work of art, music, literature, or film from your own time and place that, in your view, fits the stylistic term "baroque." Explain how and why the term is appropriate.

Chapter 21: Absolute Power and the Aristocratic Style

I. CHAPTER OBJECTIVE:

To examine the arts of the seventeenth century as expressive of absolute power and aristocratic taste

AM I FAMILIAR WITH:

- Louis XIV's Versailles as a symbol of royal absolutism and an expression of the classical baroque style?
- the main characteristics of the aristocratic style in European literature; in music; in the visual arts?
- the significance of Molière as a comic dramatist?
- how the aristocratic style manifested itself in areas beyond the West: Ottoman Turkey; Mogul India; Ming and Manchu China; Tokugawa Japan?

II. OUTLINE

A. Historical Context

   1. the Age of Absolutism

   2. the classical baroque style

B. Louis XIV and French Absolutism

   1. Versailles

   2. art patronage and the academies

   3. Poussin and academic art

   4. the aristocratic style

      a. in portraiture

      b. in European painting

   5. music and dance at Versailles

   6. neoclassicism in French literature

      a. La Rochefoucauld

      b. Molière

C. Absolutism and the Aristocratic Style beyond Europe

   1. Suleiman and the Ottoman Empire

   2. the Moguls of India

   3. China under Ming and Manchu (Qing) rule

   4. Tokugawa Japan

III. KEY TERMS: CAN I DEFINE/EXPLAIN?

(What? Why important?)

absolutism

classical baroque

château [sha TOW]

"sun king"

salon [sa LOHN]

academy

neoclassicism

maxim

comédie-ballet [KOW may dee bah LAY]

choreography

ballet

minuet [min yew ET]

aristocratic portrait

porcelain

chinoiserie [sheen waz REE]

haiku [heye koo]

shogun

samurai

kabuki [ka BOO kee]

"floating world"

Zen

IV. KEY NAMES: CAN I IDENTIFY?

(Who? What? When? Where?)

Louis XIV

Versailles [ver SAHY]

Mansart [man SAHR]

Perrault [pe ROW]

Louvre [loov]

le Vau [le VOW]

Girardon [zhi rahr DOWN]

Poussin [poo SAN]

Lorrain [low REN]

Rigaud [ree GOW]

Velásquez [vay LAS kes]

Rubens

Van Dyck

Lully [loo LEE]

Le Bourgeois Gentilhomme [le BOR zhwah jhan tee UM]

Ballet de la Nuit [bah LAY de lah NWEE]

La Rochefoucauld [la rowsh foo KOW]

Molière [mowl YER]

Suleiman [SOO lay mahn]

Safavid [SAHF ah vid]

Akbar

Jahangir [ye HAHN geer]

Shah Jahan [SHA je HAHN]

Red Fort

Taj Mahal

Agra

Ming

Manchu (Qing)

Forbidden City

Peking [pay KING]

Tokugawa [tow koo GAH wah]

Bash_ [bah SHOW]

Edo

V. KEY DATES

- 1651-1715 = rule of Louis XIV (France)
- 1648 = Louis XIV founds Academy of Painting and Sculpture
- 1669 = Louis XIV founds Academy of Music
- 1606-1627 = rule of Jahangir (India)
- 1627-1666 = rule of Shah Jahan (India)
- 1368-1644 = Ming dynasty (China)
- 1644-1911 = Qing dynasty (China)
- 1600-1868 = Tokugawa Shogunate (Japan)

VI. VOCABULARY BUILDING: CAN I DEFINE?

marquetry

aphorism

connoisseur

apotheosis

titillate

adversary

drubbing

pedagogue

VII. SAMPLE MULTIPLE CHOICE QUESTIONS

1. Louis XIV was NOT responsible for

    a. establishing the French academies.

    b. sponsoring the comedic-ballet.

    c. bringing Bernini to the court of Versailles.

    d. authorizing a new translation of the Bible.

2. The art of Poussin is representative of

    a. the rise of fresco painting.

    b. academic classicism.

    c. aristocratic portraiture.

    d. baroque illusionism.

3. *Le Bourgeois Gentilhomme* reflects Moliere's concern with social class in his portraying M. Jourdain as a man who

    a. tries desperately to assume upper class respectibility.

    b. is willing to serve the king under any circumstances.

    c. seeks to marry his daughter to a leading portrait painter.

    d. commissions a magnificent tomb for his deceased wife.

4. Known as "the Magnificent," _____ ruled over the Ottoman Empire and encouraged a golden age of literature and art.

    a. Akbar

    b. Suleiman

    c. Shah Jahan

    d. Jahangir

5. Shared by the seventeenth-century aristocratic courts of France, India, China, and Japan was the

    a. production of comic opera and ballet.

    b. commissioning of extravagant royal palaces.

    c. effort to make cultural contact with each other.

    d. will to employ the arts as expressive of mass sentiments.

(Answers appear on page x.)

VIII. ESSAY QUESTIONS/WRITING EXERCISE

1. Describe in your own words the major features of the aristocratic style. What function(s) did it serve? In your view, which art works in this chapter best reflect this style?

2. The gap between the ruler and the ruled is an underlying theme in this chapter. Did the arts of the period serve to widen or narrow the gap? Does Molière offer any perspective on this matter?

3. Define "classical baroque" as a style. How did it differ from the baroque style discussed in Chapter 20? Cite examples.

4. What similarities and differences do you detect between the aristocratic art of seventeenth-century France, India, and China?

IX. MAKING CONNECTIONS

1. Locate an architectural example of "the aristocratic style" in your own town or city. What kind of public events are held in this environment? In what ways does the decor contribute to an elitist style?

2. Was there an aristocratic style elsewhere in the seventeenth-century world, such as in Africa or the Americas?

3. Visit a local art museum, bank, or university administative building that houses portraits of notable individuals. What features of the aristocratic style are evident in these portraits?

4. Obtain and view a video of *The Last Emperor* (1987, directed by Bernardo Bertolucci). Based on the visual data provided in the film, describe your impressions of China's Forbidden City.

5. Investigate: How did the "garden plan" seen at Versailles influence the city plans of Paris and Washington, D.C.?

Chapter 22: The Baroque in the Protestant North

I. CHAPTER OBJECTIVE:

To survey the arts of Northern Europe as expressive of Protestant religious devotionalism

AM I FAMILIAR WITH:

- the literary achievements of Donne and Milton?
- the unique characteristics of Protestant devotionalism as reflected in the art of Rembrandt?
- the religious compositions of Handel and Bach?
- the role of the Bible in the arts of the seventeenth century?

II. OUTLINE

A. Historical Context for the Protestant North

    1. the shaping influence of the Bible

    2. the English Commonwealth

    3. the dominance of the middle class

B. Baroque Literature in Northern Europe

    1. King James Bible

    2. Donne and metaphysical poetry

    3. Milton and Paradise Lost

C. Baroque Art and Music in Northern Europe

    1. Wren and Saint Paul's Cathedral

    2. Rembrandt and devotionalism

    3. Handel and the oratorio

    4. Bach and religious music

III. KEY TERMS: CAN I DEFINE/EXPLAIN?

(What? Why important?)

pietism [PEYE i tiz em]

metaphysical poetry

conceit

etching

intaglio [in TAH lyow]

burin [BYOOR in]

impasto [im PAS tow]

homophony [how MOF ah nee]

figured bass

cantata [con TAH ta]

oratorio [orah TOR ee oh]

prelude

IV. KEY NAMES/CAN I IDENTIFY?

(Who? What? When? Where?

Charles I of England

James II of England

Van Dyck [van DEYK]

Glorious Revolution

Douay [doo AY]

Donne

Milton

Paradise Lost

Rembrandt

Amsterdam

"Hundred Guilder Print"

Handel

Messiah

J.S. Bach [BAHK]

V. KEY DATES

- 1611 = King James Version of the Bible published
- 1642-1658 = English Civil War
- 1688 = Glorious Revolution; English Bill of Rights

VI. VOCABULARY BUILDING/CAN I DEFINE?

paradoxical

proletarian

guilder

Passion

VII. SAMPLE MULTIPLE CHOICE QUESTIONS

1. Metaphysical poetry depends largely on the use of

   a. arias and recitatives.

   b. complex images known as "conceits."

   c. neoplatonic references.

   d. all of these.

2. John Donne was NOT

   a. dean of Saint Paul's Cathedral.

   b. a writer of eloquent sermons.

   c. the architect of Saint Paul's Cathedral.

   d. a writer of sonnets.

3. *Paradise Lost* reflects John Milton's close familiarity with

   a. the King James Bible.

   b. the works of Shakespeare.

   c. the English Civil War.

   d. all of the above.

4. Rembrandt's etchings were especially popular among the

   a. Dutch royalists.

   b. middle class.

   c. aristocracy.

   d. church officials.

5. Handel's *Messiah* is a(n)

   a. cantata.

   b. oratorio.

   c. opera.

   d. prelude.

(Answers appear on page x.)

VIII. VISUAL/SPATIAL EXERCISE

In the space below, COMPARE the movements and styles examined in Chapters 20, 21, and 22, citing specific examples for each. Full sentences are not necessary.

CATHOLIC REFORMATION BAROQUE   BAROQUE IN THE PROTESTANT NORTH

Religious Factors/Events: Religious Factors/Events:

Literature: Literature:

Architecture: Architecture:

Sculpture/Painting: Sculpture/Painting:

Music: Music:

IX. ESSAY QUESTIONS/WRITING EXERCISE

1. What is the theme of Milton's *Paradise Lost?* Who are the central characters? Which aspects of the epic may be considered "baroque"? Which are expressive of Protestant devotionalism?

2. Discuss the Bible as a shaping influence on the literature, art, and music of seventeenth-century Europe.

3. Do you find the literature, art, and music discussed in this chapter more or less "theatrical" than that in Chapter 20? If so, how so? If not, how not?

4. Why are Milton, Rembrandt, and Bach considered major figures in the arts of the Western world?

X .MAKING CONNECTIONS

1. What religious scripture was followed in your home or place of worship when you were a child? Did its use have an affect on you in the course of your personal development?

2. Prepare a screenplay (film or TV) for the portion of Milton's *Paradise Lost* that appears in the textbook. What aspects of the subject might be most interesting to a modern audience?

3. Attend a live performance of *Messiah*. What parts did you find most compelling? Why?

Chapter 23: The Scientific Revolution and the New Learning

I. CHAPTER OBJECTIVE:

To examine the cultural and intellectual impact of the Scientific Revolution and the New Learning in the West

AM I FAMILIAR WITH:

- the central figures of the Scientific Revolution (Copernicus, Kepler, Galileo, Newton) and their contributions?
- the fundamental ideas of Bacon, Descartes, and Locke?
- the difference between inductive and deductive reasoning?
- the impact of the Scientific Revolution on European art and music?

II. OUTLINE

   A. The Scientific Revolution

       1. sixteenth-century background

       2. Kepler and Galileo

       3. religious opposition

       4. scientific instruments and methods

   B. The New Learning

       1. Bacon and inductive reasoning

       2. Descartes and deductive reasoning

       3. the challenge to traditional religion

       4. Locke and the empirical tradition

       5. the Newtonian synthesis

   C. Impact of Science and the New Learning on the Arts

       1. Northern baroque painting

          a. still life

          b. genre painting

          c. Vermeer and Dutch art

          d. Rembrandt and Dutch portraiture

       2. Instrumental Music

          a. improvements in instruments

          b. the rise of new instrumental forms

          c. Vivaldi

          d. J.S. Bach

III. KEY TERMS: CAN I DEFINE/EXPLAIN?

(What? Why important?)

scientia [shee EN chyah]

geocentric theory

heliocentric theory

empirical method

inductive reasoning

deductive reasoning

idols

Cogito ergo sum [KOW gee tow ER gow SUM]

tabula rasa [TAH boo lah RAH zah]

deism [DEE izm]

genre painting

vanitas [VAN ee tahs]

camera obscura [KA me rah ob SKOO rah]

concerto grosso [con CHER tow GROW sow]

sonata

fugue

suite [SWEET]

IV. KEY NAMES: CAN I IDENTIFY?

(Who? What? When? Where?)

Vesalius

Copernicus

Kepler

Galileo

Bruno [BROO no]

Bacon

Novum Organum [NO vum or GAN um]

Descartes [day KAHRT]

Spinoza [spi NO zah]

Pascal [pas KAL]

Locke

Newton

de Heem

van Oosterwyck [fon OOST er vik]

de Hooch [de HOOK]

ter Borch [tur BOWRK]

Vermeer [ver MIR]

Rembrandt

Hals [HAHLS]

Leyster [LEYE sta]

Vivaldi [vi VAHL dee]

Art of the Fugue

Brandenburg Concertos

V. KEY DATES

- 1543 = Copernicus publishes *On the Revolution of the Heavenly Spheres*
- 1608 = invention of the telescope
- 1620 = Bacon publishes the *Novum Organum*
- 1632 = Rembrandt completes *The Anatomy Lesson of Dr. Tulp*
- 1687 = Newton publishes the *Principia Mathematica*
- 1721 = Bach dedicates the *Brandenburg Concertos*

VI. VOCABULARY BUILDING: CAN I DEFINE?

alchemy

axiom

convivial

VII. SAMPLE MULTIPLE CHOICE QUESTIONS

1. _____ was forced by the church to recant his own scientific findings.

   a. Copernicus

   b. Kepler

   c. Galileo

   d. Newton

2. The music of the seventeenth century is characterized by

   a. the rise of purely instrumental compositions.

   b. refinements in the tuning of musical instruments.

   c. an interest in programmatic music.

   d. all of these.

3. The Scientific Revolution influenced seventeenth-century prose by its

   a. emphasis on precise expression and factual detail.

   b. new affirmation of equality of the sexes.

   c. exaltation of free speech.

   d. high regard for lyric poetry with complex phrasing.

4. Locke's conception of the *tabula rasa*

   a. confirms Descartes' claim, "I think, therefore I am."

   b. suggests that human knowledge derives from sensory experience.

   c. affirms Bacon's description of the Idol of the Cave.

   d. supports Pascal's view of the spiritual quest for God.

5. One of the key features of seventeenth-century Dutch painting was

   a. a renewed concern for classical allegory.

   b. the successful depiction of light.

   c. portraits that flattered the aristocracy.

   d. a dislike for realistic detail.

(Answers appear on page x.)

VIII. ESSAY QUESTIONS/WRITING EXERCISE

1. Citing specific examples from this chapter, describe the impact of the Scientific Revolution on the visual arts of the seventeenth century.

2. In what ways do the musical developments of the baroque North reflect a new direction in Western musical tradition? Cite specific examples.

3. Examine the ways in which Dutch still life paintings reflect the values of their time and place.

4. How do the portraits of Vermeer, Rembrandt, Hals, and Leyster differ from the portraits illustrated in Chapter 21?

IX. MAKING CONNECTIONS

1. Explain the nature of each of Bacon's Idols in your own words, giving an example of your own (or others') "errors" in perception and understanding that illustrates each..

2. Make a case FOR Descartes' proposition, "I think, therefore I am." Now make an equally convincing case AGAINST this proposition.

3. Which of the paintings illustrated in Chapter 23 is the most "true to life"? Why so? Which looks most like a photograph? How so? Compare photographic portraiture with painted portraits of your own family. Is the photograph always "truer-to-life?"

X. BONUS

TEXTURES

| Monophonic | One Melody (unaccompanied) | |

Homophonic		
Melody (one voice or line)		
Chordal accompaniment (several voices in harmony)		

Polyphonic		free counterpoint
Imitative counterpoint A four-voice fugue	Fugue subject (voice 1)	
	Subject imitated in voice 2	
	Imitated in voice 3	
	Imitated in voice 4	

Non-imitative counterpoint with all melodies being of equal importance		
Voice 1		
Voice 2		
Voice 3		

XI. SYNTHESIS/PART I: THE AGE OF THE BAROQUE

Review the Introduction to Book 4, Part I (page 1) before beginning this exercise. Choose ONE of the following as the subject for an extended essay:

1. The baroque has been called a theatrical style, one that deals in spectacle, grandeur, and dramatic contrast. Test these concepts in an essay that discusses the baroque as an expression of the Catholic Reformation, Protestant Devotionalism, the Scientific Revolution, and the Age of Absolutism. Defend your general statements with specific examples.

2. Opera is usually regarded as the quintessential baroque artform. Why so? Which works of art, music, or literature (in chapters 20-23) seem to you most expressive of the baroque spirit?

3. Discuss the increasing visibility of women in the Age of the Baroque. Make specific reference to primary texts in your discussion.

4. Assess the differences between European culture and those of the East (India, China, and Japan) during the seventeenth century. Can one reliably apply the word "baroque" to describe the arts of any non-European culture?

5. Among the readings in this unit, "The Age of the Baroque," which one would you select if you were assigned to read the entire work. Why?

PART II: THE AGE OF ENLIGHTENMENT

Chapter 24: The Promise of Reason

I. CHAPTER OBJECTIVE:

To explore the European Enlightenment as a movement that emphasized social progress and human perfectibility

AM I FAMILIAR WITH:

- the political views of Hobbes and Locke?
- how Smith, Diderot, Condorcet, and Wollstonecraft help to shape the concepts of social and economic progress?
- the impact of the Enlightenment on European literature?

II. OUTLINE

A. Historical Context for the Enlightenment

    1. the impact of the Scientific Revolution

    2. the growing middle class

    3. rising literacy

B. The Social Order and Natural Law

    1. the concept of natural law

    2. political theories of Hobbes and Locke

    3. Locke's influence on Montesquieu and Jefferson

    4. Smith and economic theory

C. The *Philosophes*

    1. the role of the *salon*

    2. Diderot and the *Encyclopédie*

    3. encyclopedic literature

    4. concepts of social progress: Condorcet and Wollstonecraft

    5. impact on literature

        a. the journalistic essay

        b. the novel

        c. the poetry of Alexander Pope

III. KEY TERMS: CAN I DEFINE/EXPLAIN?

(What? Why important?)

salon [se LOHN]

natural law

philosophe [fee low ZUF]

laissez-faire economics [les ay FAYR]

social contract

Enlightenment

deism

philosophic optimism

principle of sufficient reason

journalistic essay

broadsheet

periodical

novel

heroic couplet

Leviathan

IV. KEY NAMES: CAN I IDENTIFY?

(Who? What? When? Where?)

Hobbes

Locke

Montesquieu [mahn tes KYOO]

Jefferson

Smith

Diderot [dee de ROW]

Encyclopédie [akin see klow pay DEE]

Leibnitz [LEYEB nitz]

Beccaria [be KAHR ee ah]

Condorcet [kahn dowr SAY]

Wollstonecraft

Johnson

Gibbon

Addison

Steele

Defoe

Fielding

Pope

V. KEY DATES

- 1651 = Hobbes publishes the *Leviathan*
- 1687 = Newton publishes the *Principia Mathematica*
- 1690 = Locke publishes the *First Treatise on Government*
- 1751-1772 = Diderot publishes the *Encyclopédie*
- 1776 = America adopts the Declaration of Independence

VI. VOCABULARY BUILDING: CAN I DEFINE?

commodious

sovereign

commonwealth

tyranny

invidious

dispel

vindication

VII. SAMPLE MULTIPLE CHOICE QUESTIONS

1. The social science known as sociology is associated with the name

    a. Locke.

    b. Hobbes.

    c. Montesquieu.

    d. Condorcet.

2. According to Hobbes society must submit to rule by a strong individual because

    a. divine right kingship is sanctioned by the Bible.

    b. people are by nature warlike and selfish.

    c. societies become corrupt as they mature.

    d. all of these.

3. NOT a dominant form of literary expression in the seventeenth century:

    a. journalistic essay

    b. historical narrative

    c. novel

    d. lyric poetry

4. The French salon, center of intellectual debate, was usually organized by

   a. noblewomen.

   b. royalty.

   c. political leaders.

   d. members of the literary academy.

5. The line "A mighty maze! but not without a plan" reflects Pope's argument that

   a. morality is based in human willpower.

   b. nature is rational but divinely ordered.

   c. human progress is inevitable.

   d. education in Greek and Latin are essential.

(Answers appear on page x.)

VIII. VISUAL/SPATIAL EXERCISE

In the GRAPHIC CLUSTER on the next page write freely to summarize the contributions of key Enlightenment figures and to explore the basic concepts associated with the European Enlightenment. You may write within or across the "windows" of the cluster.

THE PROMISE OF REASON

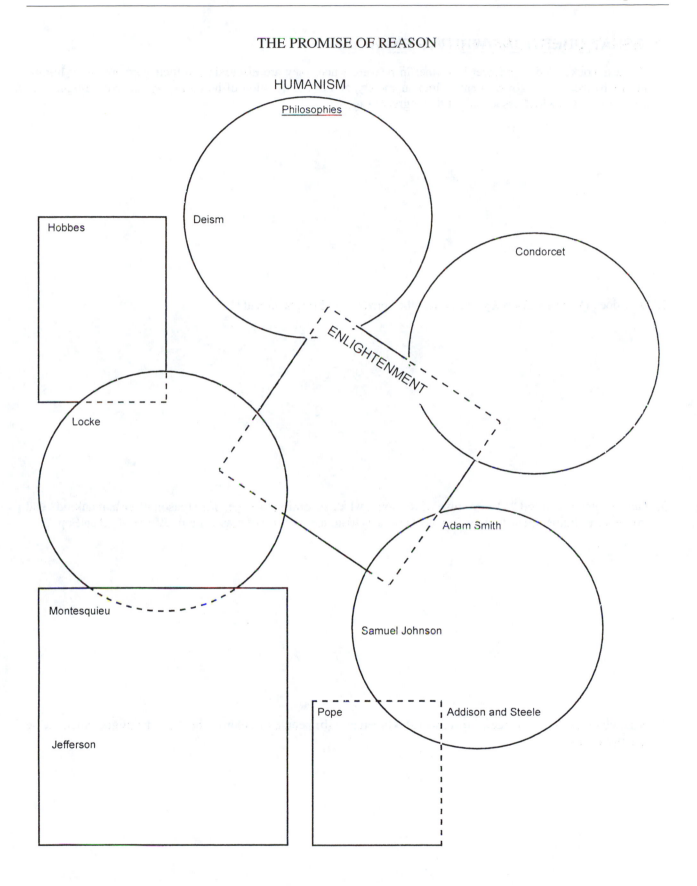

HUMANISM

Philosophies

Deism

Hobbes

Condorcet

ENLIGHTENMENT

Locke

Adam Smith

Montesquieu

Samuel Johnson

Jefferson

Pope

Addison and Steele

IX. ESSAY QUESTIONS/WRITING EXERCISE

1. Hobbes, Locke, and Condorcet have met in heaven, where they are discussing a) their perceptions of human nature, b) the role of government in human society, and c) the question of human progress. What might each have to say? On which issues might they agree/disagree?

2. How does Diderot's *Encyclopédie* reflect the spirit of the Enlightenment?

3. This chapter is entitled "The Promise of Reason"; what, according to Pope, does reason offer humankind? Did any other Enlightenment figures, in your view, articulate the promise of reason more effectively than Pope?

4. What changes do you perceive towards (a) women and (b) people of color in the Age of Enlightenment? Cite specific examples.

X. MAKING CONNECTIONS

1. Update the encyclopedia entry for "Negroes" found in Chapter 24. What would you add or delete to modernize the entry?

2. Describe an event or enterprise (in which you were involved), the success of which depended exclusively on the exercise of reason.

3. How many of Pope's basic views on nature and humankind (Reading 4.21) do you share? With which would you take issue? Why?

4. Research Jefferson's views on Blacks based on his own writings and the evidence of his personal and political life.

5. Evaluate Mary Wollstonecraft's *Vindication of the Rights of Women* from a twenty-first century perspective.

Chapter 25: The Limits of Reason

I. CHAPTER OBJECTIVE:

To assess the limitations of Enlightenment ambitions as reflected in eighteenth-century culture

AM I FAMILIAR WITH:

- the purpose and the nature of transatlantic slave trade?
- the role of satire as an instrument for attacking false values?
- Voltaire's *Candide* as literary satire?
- the revolt against reason in the writings of Rousseau and Kant?
- the reasons for and consequences of the revolutions in America and in France?

II. OUTLINE

A. Historical Context for the Eighteenth Century

    1. reactions against Enlightenment rationalism

    2. the consequences of European industrialism

    3. the transatlantic slave trade: Equiano's *Travels*

B. Satire: Weapon of the Enlightenment

    1. European literature: Goldsmith and Swift

    2. satire in China

    3. Voltaire's *Candide*

    4. the visual arts: Hogarth

C. The Revolt Against Reason

    1. Rousseau

    2. Kant

D. Late Eighteenth-Century Revolutions

    1. in North America

    2. in France

III. KEY TERMS: CAN I DEFINE/EXPLAIN?

(What? Why important?)

transatlantic slave trade

irony

philosophic idealism

noble savage

engraving

caricature

categorical imperative

transcendental idealism

Third Estate

Bastille [bah STEEL]

IV. KEY NAMES: CAN I IDENTIFY?

(Who? What? When? Where?)

Equiano [ek wee AH now]

Wheatley

Swift

Voltaire [vahl TER]

Candide

Pangloss

Cunegonde [coo ne GAHN dah]

Li Ruzhen [LEE JOO CHEN]

Hogarth

Rousseau [roo SOW]

Émile

Hume

Kant [KAHNT]

Paine

de Gouges [de GOOJ]

V. KEY DATES

- 1726 = Swift publishes *Gulliver's Travels*
- 1755 = Lisbon earthquake
- 1759 = Voltaire publishes *Candide*
- 1781 = Kant publishes the *Critique of Pure Reason*
- 1789 = ratification of the Constitution of the United States of America
- 1789 = storming of the Bastille in Paris
- 1794 = Louis XVI beheaded

VI. VOCABULARY BUILDING: CAN I DEFINE?

alleviate

venereal

vernacular

paranoia

papist

VII. SAMPLE MULTIPLE CHOICE QUESTIONS

1. Swift's *Modest Proposal* resembles Li Ruzhen's *Flowers in the Mirror* in its satirization of

   a. false religious beliefs.

   b. physical exploitation.

   c. the brutal treatment of slaves.

   d. philosophic optimism.

2. In Voltaire's *Candide,* the character Pangloss is modeled on

   a. Leibniz.

   b. Louis XIV.

   c. Condorcet.

   d. Hobbes.

3. The visual satires of William Hogarth were

   a. inspired by British stage comedies.

   b. paintings reproduced as engravings.

   c. pointed attacks on British poverty and alcoholism.

   d. all of the above.

4. Rousseau held that

   a. societies begin by defining property rights.

   b. societies work towards improving human beings.

   c. societies move toward increased social equality.

   d. all of the above.

5. The revolutions of the late eighteenth century

   a. were basically unsuccessful.

   b. took place in almost every part of Europe.

   c. put Enlightenment idealism into action.

   d. inspired great works of satire.

(Answers appear on page x.)

VIII. VISUAL/SPATIAL EXERCISE

Geography of Seventeenth- and Eighteenth-Century Europe

On the map below, locate and label the following places:

Genoa	Austria	Delft	Lisbon
Ireland	Madrid	Holy Roman Empire	Scotland
Rome	Netherlands	North Sea	Berlin
Poland	Vienna	Adriatic Sea	
London	France	Erfurt	

IX. ESSAY QUESTIONS/WRITING EXERCISE

1. Voltaire mocks the notions that love is ennobling and that warfare is a glorious endeavor; what other traditional attitudes and beliefs does Voltaire attack in *Candide?* Do Swift and Hogarth also mock human behavior? How so?

2. Satire is said to bring attention to contradictions between the ideal and the real. What social and historical conditions inspired the satirists of the eighteenth century? Why, in your view, were there no satires of the conditions described by Equiano (Reading 4.22)?

3. What were Rousseau's major criticisms of society and education? What reforms did he envision?

4. Identify any three of the following phrases, and comment briefly on each:

   (a) "All of the events in this best of [all] possible worlds are admirably connected."

   (b) "Where there is no property, there is no injury."

   (c) "Act as if the maxim of your action should become the law for all humankind."

   (d) "Liberty, Equality, Fraternity."

X. MAKING CONNECTIONS

1. Write a satire bringing to public view the injustices of the transatlantic slave trade as described in Equiano's *Travels* (Reading 4.22).

2. Find an editorial cartoon that attacks a contemporary social problem or institution. Are cartoons as effective as literary satire? Why or why not?

3. In your view, should all humans "be forced to be free" (as Rousseau suggests)? Why or why not?

4. Examine the interface between liberty (as Enlightenment writers perceived it) and women's rights. Did Enlightenment thinkers perceive women as possessing natural rights?

Chapter 26: Eighteenth-Century Art, Music, and Society

I. CHAPTER OBJECTIVE:

To appreciate the arts of the eighteenth century in relation to changing values and tastes in Western society

AM I FAMILIAR WITH:

- the rococo style as an expression of upper-class taste?
- the development of genre realism and neoclassicism as stylistic alternatives to the rococo?
- neoclassicism as a vehicle for noble idealism and authority in Western art?
- the major developments in eighteenth-century music: the birth of the orchestra and new forms of classical composition?

II. OUTLINE

A. The Rococo Style

    1. historical context: France

    2. in Austria and Bavaria

    3. French rococo painting

        a. Watteau

        b. Boucher

        c. Vigée-Lebrun

        d. Fragonard

    4. French rococo sculpture

B. Genre Painting

    1. as reaction against rococo

    2. Greuze and Chardin

C. Neoclassicism

    1. the new archeology

    2. as expression of Enlightenment ideals

    3. architecture

        a. Soufflot

        b. Jefferson

        c. Gibbs

    4. sculpture

        a. Canova

        b. Houdon

        c. Wedgwood

5. painting

   a. David

   b. Ingres

   c. Kauffmann

6. Neoclassicism under Napoleon

D. Eighteenth-Century Music

1. rococo music

2. classical music

3. birth of the orchestra

4. classical instrumental forms

5. the classical style

   a. Haydn

   b. Mozart

   c. early Beethoven

III. KEY TERMS: CAN I DEFINE/EXPLAIN?

(What? Why important?)

rococo

neoclassicism

fête galante [fet gah LANT]

pastel

satyr

bacchante [bah KAHNT]

symphony

score

string quartet

sonata

sonata form

allegro [ah LAY grow]

andante [ahn DAHN tay]

coda

concerto

fortissimo [for TEES ee mow]

largo [LAHR gow]

opera buffa [OW pe rah BOO fa]

woodwinds

brass

strings

percussion

IV. KEY NAMES: CAN I IDENTIFY?

(Who? What? When? Where?)

Ottobeuren [ah tow boy ren]

Fischer

Watteau [wah TOW]

Boucher [boo SHAY]

Vigée-Lebrun [vee JAY le BRUN]

Fragonard [fra gow NAHR]

Madame de Pompadour

Marie Antoinette [an twan NET]

Clodion [CLOW dee on]

Greuze [GROOZ]

Chardin [shahr DAN]

Piranesi

Winckelmann [VEEN kel mahn]

Herculaneum and Pompeii

Soufflot [soo FLOW]

Canova [kah NO vain]

Gibbs

Wedgwood

Houdon

Jefferson

David [dah VEED]

Ingres [ANG ru]

Horatii [hor AY see eye]

Arc de Triomphe [tree UMPH]

Couperin [koop RAN]

Stamitz [STAM its]

Haydn [HEYE den]

Mozart [MOWT zahrt]

V. KEY DATES

- 1738 = first archeological excavations of Herculaneum
- 1782 = David completes the *Oath of the Horatii*
- 1790 = Haydn invited to perform in London
- 1799 = Napoleon seizes control of the French government

VI. VOCABULARY BUILDING: CAN I DEFINE?

undulating

rustic

dictum

ephemeral

odalisque

VII. SAMPLE MULTIPLE CHOICE QUESTIONS

1. The rococo style reflects the influence of the decorative arts of

    a. India.

    b. China.

    c. Africa.

    d. all of the above.

2. The woman who influenced the commercial popularity of Sèvres porcelain and commissioned Boucher to paint her portrait was

    a. Madame de Pompadour.

    b. Marie Antoinette.

    c. the Marquise du Châtelet.

    d. Elizabeth Vigée-Lebrun.

3. NOT generally considered a painter of the rococo style:

    a. Fragonard

    b. Boucher

    c. Greuze

    d. Watteau

4. Neoclassical art and classical music have in common an emphasis on

    a. clarity and formal structure.

    b. biblical themes.

    c. freedom of form.

    d. all of the above.

5. Eighteenth-century musical developments included all EXCEPT which one of the following?

    a. new forms of instrumental music

    b. the birth of the symphony orchestra

    c. the use of the sonata form

    d. the birth of opera and oratorio

(Answers appear on page x.)

VIII. ESSAY QUESTIONS/WRITING EXERCISE

1. How did the paintings of Greuze and Chardin differ from those of Watteau, Boucher, and Fragonard? How did those of David differ from the paintings of all of the above artists?

2. What do we mean by "classical music"? By "the classical style" in music? Cite specific examples.

3. Find and describe some examples of the neoclassical heritage in American architecture and popular culture. Begin by examining the monuments and buildings in your own city or town, then look beyond local and regional areas.

IX. MAKING CONNECTIONS

1. On a CD or in live performance, listen to a complete symphony by Haydn or Mozart. Which of the *visual* illustrations in chapter 26 come closest to capturing your *listening* experience? How so?

2. Is there in America today such a thing as upper class art or music; middle class art or music; lower class art or music? If you believe so, explain and suggest examples of each.

3. You are designing the main living area for your country estate.. Which style do you prefer: that illustrated in Figure 26.1 or that illustrated in Figure 26.17? Explain the reasons for your selection.

4. Draft a contemporary version of Mozart's *Marriage of Figaro*. (It may be rap, rock, hip-hop, etc.).

X. SYNTHESIS/PART II: THE AGE OF ENLIGHTENMENT

Write an extended essay on any ONE of the following:

1. How did the arts of the eighteenth century reflect the ideals of the European Enlightenment? In your answer, you may wish to examine specific works in terms of text, context, and subtext.

2. In the seventeenth and eighteenth centuries, the West generated some of the most long-lasting ideas and art forms of the early modern era. Isolate and discuss those you believe are most significant.

3. What aspects of Enlightenment thought and culture still influence your everyday life or your basic social and political views?

4. Which of the artists and composers in these chapters "spoke for" or represented the values of the upper class? Which represented middle- and lower-class values? Does the art and music each produced, nevertheless have universal or enduring appeal? If so, why so?

5. Make a case FOR the claim that human history is progressive and that day-to-day life has gradually improved. Then make an equally convincing case AGAINST these propositions.

BOOK 5
ROMANTICISM, REALISM, AND THE NINETEENTH-CENTURY WORLD

PART I: THE ROMANTIC ERA

Chapter 27: The Romantic View of Nature

I. CHAPTER OBJECTIVE:

To examine the romantic view of nature as reflected in the nineteenth-century world

AM I FAMILIAR WITH:

- the European romantic poets and their attitudes towards nature?
- attitudes toward nature in Asian culture; Native American culture?
- the rise of the romantic landscape in Western art?
- transcendentalism and other views of nature in nineteenth-century America?
- the intellectual contributions of Hegel and Darwin?

II. OUTLINE

A. Historical Context

    1. economic and social conditions

    2. birth of European romanticism

B. Nature and the Natural in European Literature

    1. Wordsworth

    2. Shelley

    3. Keats

C. Nature and the Natural in Asian Literature

    1. Chinese nature poetry and landscape art

    2. Shen Fu and Chinese prose

D. Romantic Landscape Painting

    1. Constable

    2. Turner

    3. Friedrich

    4. Corot

E. Romanticism in America

    1. Transcendentalism

        a. Emerson

        b. Thoreau

    2. Walt Whitman

    3. moralizing landscapes

    4. Native American arts and nature

    5. American folk art

E. Nature and Intellectual Thought

    1. Schopenhauer

    2. romantic mysticism

    3. Hegel

    4. Darwin and evolution

III. KEY TERMS: CAN I DEFINE/EXPLAIN?

(What? Why important?)

industrialism

nationalism

romanticism

metaphor

assonance

tone

color

ode

transcendentalism

mysticism

natural selection

evolution

"survival of the fittest"

free verse

Hegelian dialectic

"scientism"

social Darwinism

IV. KEY NAMES: CAN I IDENTIFY?

(Who? What? When? Where?)

Wordsworth

Coleridge

Tintern Abbey

Shelley

Keats [KEETS]

Shen Fu

Six Chapters from a Floating Life

Constable

Turner

Friedrich [FREED rik]

Barbizon

Corot [kow ROW]

Emerson

Thoreau

Walden

Whitman

Cole

Bierstadt [BIR shtat]

Church

Catlin

Hegel [HAY gul]

Schopenhauer [SHOW pen hou er]

Novalis [now VAL es]

Darwin

V. KEY DATES

- 1800 = second edition of the *Lyrical Ballads*
- 1845 = Thoreau settles at Walden Pond
- 1859 = Darwin publishes *The Origin of Species*

VI. VOCABULARY BUILDING: CAN I DEFINE?

paean

atheism

pantheistic

panorama

malignant

euphoric

VII. SAMPLE MULTIPLE CHOICE QUESTIONS

1. The landmark work that marked the birth of the romantic movement was

   a. *The Origin of Species.*

   b. *Leaves of Grass.*

   c. *Defence of Poetry.*

   d. *Lyrical Ballads.*

2. Free verse is a form of poetry that

   a. breaks with traditional meter.

   b. was explored by Whitman.

   c. is closely tied to natural verbal expression.

   d. all of the above.

3. All except which of the following romantics were British:

   a. Friedrich

   b. Constable

   c. Shelley

   d. Turner

4. Wordsworth's perception of nature as sublime was most closely echoed in the paintings of

   a. Corot.

   b. Catlin.

   c. Turner.

   d. Cole.

5. Transcendentalism

   a. began in England and traveled to America.

   b. valued intuition and self-reliance.

   c. rejected Christian teachings in favor of Eastern religions.

   d. all of the above.

(Answers appear on page x.)

VIII. VISUAL/SPATIAL EXERCISE

In the GRAPHIC CLUSTER on the next page, write freely the ideas you associate with the phrases in each of the "windows."

THE ROMANTIC VIEW OF NATURE

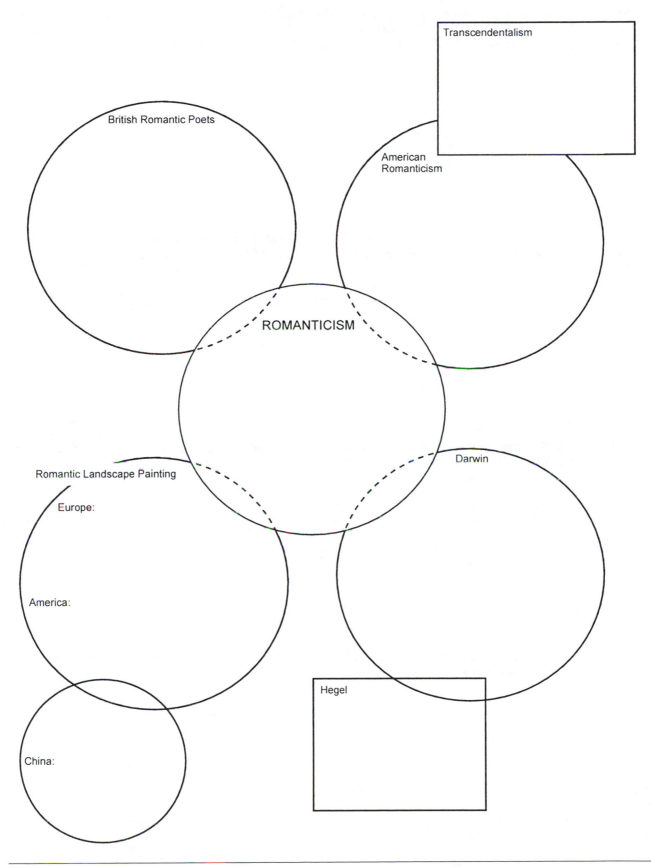

Transcendentalism

British Romantic Poets

American Romanticism

ROMANTICISM

Romantic Landscape Painting

Europe:

America:

China:

Darwin

Hegel

IX. ESSAY QUESTIONS/WRITING EXERCISE

1. Identify and discuss the following lines of poetry, showing how each reflects the romantic attitude toward nature: "Nature never did betray/ The heart that loved her"; "If Winter comes, can Spring be far behind?" "'Beauty is truth, truth beauty,'—that is all/ Ye know on earth, and all ye need to know."

2. In what ways is Shen Fu's autobiography "romantic"? How does it compare with British romantic literature? Are there similar differences between European landscape art and Chinese landscape art?

3. In what ways does the romanticism of Thoreau and Whitman differ from that of Wordsworth, Shelley, and Keats? Can similar distinctions be made between British and American landscape painting?

4. Write an essay on the subject of "the individual and nature" based on your responses to any of the figures in this chapter that depict people in a landscape setting.

X. MAKING CONNECTIONS

1. Would you consider your personal view of nature "romantic"? If so, how so? If not, why not?

2. Consider the "new age" movements to "save the earth" and the ecologically oriented views of planet Earth as a holistic entity. Are these movements/views fundamentally romantic? If so, how so?

3. If you had a choice of owning a romantic landscape painting or a piece of Zuni pottery, which would you choose? Why?

4. Make a visit to a lake, mountain, or other natural site; write a poem that expresses your personal responses to the sounds, smells, and sights of this particular setting.

Chapter 28: The Romantic Hero

I. CHAPTER OBJECTIVE:

To examine the romantic significance of historical and fictional heroes and heroines in nineteenth-century Western culture

AM I FAMILIAR WITH:

- the role and influence of nationalism in the romantic era
- the concept of the heroic personality as manifested in the fictional figures of Prometheus, Frankenstein, and Faust?
- the significance of historical heroes (such as Napoleon and Douglass) in nineteenth-century culture?
- nineteenth-century romantic stereotypes of the female?

II. OUTLINE

A. Nationalism and the Romantic Hero

    1. liberty and nationalistic sentiment

    2. nineteenth-century hero worship

    3. Rousseau's influence

B. The Romantic Hero

    1. traditional stereotypes versus historical heroes: Napoleon

    2. Prometheus

        a. Mary Shelley

        b. Byron

        c. Pushkin

    3. American abolitionism

        a. Douglass

        b. Sojourner Truth

        c. Slave songs and spirituals

    4. Goethe's *Faust*

C. The Romantic Heroine

    1. popular stereotypes

    2. Sand and other female writers

III. KEY TERMS: CAN I DEFINE/EXPLAIN?

(What? Why important?)

nationalism

Promethean

abolitionism

slave songs

stereotype

Byronic

femme fatale [fam fey TAHL]

Faustian

IV. KEY NAMES: CAN I IDENTIFY?

(Who? What? When? Where?)

Napoleon

Prometheus [prow MEE thee us]

Byron

Pushkin

Mary Shelley

Frankenstein

Douglass

Sojourner Truth

Goethe [GUR te]

Faust

Mephistopheles [me fi STAHF u leez]

Heine [HEYE ne]

Bizet [bee ZAY]

George Eliot

Jane Austen

George Sand

V. KEY DATES

- 1804 = Napoleon proclaims himself emperor
- 1812 = Napoleon invades Russia
- 1832 = Goethe completes *Faust*
- 1855 = Douglass writes *My Bondage and My Freedom*

VI. VOCABULARY BUILDING: CAN I DEFINE?

egocentric

tenacity

ruminations

unrequited

bohemian

voluptuous

whence

phenomena

antebellum

VII. SAMPLE MULTIPLE CHOICE QUESTIONS

1. In his diary, Napoleon places great emphasis on the power of

    a. his army.

    b. religious inspiration.

    c. imagination.

    d. university education.

2. Prometheus was a favorite fictional hero because

    a. he defied the Greek gods.

    b. he risked losing his soul to gain knowledge.

    c. he was transformed into a monster.

    d. all of the above.

3. Pushkin's general attitude toward Napoleon:

    a. condemnation for his bravado

    b. admiration for his heroic actions

    c. disapproval of his political policies

    d. anger at his ultimate failure

4. In *My Bondage and My Freedom,* Douglass confesses that he stole food

    a. on the grounds of morality.

    b. as an act of revenge against his master.

    c. because other slaves did so.

    d. on a misguided impulse.

5. Prior to signing a pact with the devil, Faust tries to gain knowledge through

    a. completing degrees in Law and Medicine.

    b. mastering the art of black magic.

    c. studying theology.

    d. all of the above.

6. The stereotype of the female LEAST often presented by nineteenth-century male writers pictured womankind as

    a. jealous and seductive.

    b. procreative and nurturing.

    c. independent-minded.

    d. angelic and chaste.

(Answers appear on page x.)

VIII. VISUAL/SPATIAL EXERCISE

On the map below, locate and label the following places:

Austria	Paris	Russia	Portugal
Warsaw	Prussia	Norway	Rhine River
Madrid	Corsica	Naples	
Barcelona	Elba	London	

IX. ESSAY QUESTIONS/WRITING EXERCISE

1. Choose one historical and one fictional nineteenth-century hero and explain why each appealed to the romantic imagination of the time. Cite examples from the chapter.

2. In what ways might the Frankenstein story be considered the quintessential romantic story? Why has it continued to capture the imagination into our own time?

3. Compare Faust with those heroes that you have encountered in other works of literature, such as Gilgamesh, Achilles, Roland, Lancelot, and Hamlet. In what ways is this figure similar? In what ways different?

4. In what ways did nationalism influence the character and the development of nineteenth-century romanticism?

X. MAKING CONNECTIONS

1. In what ways do America's current TV and film heroes (e.g., Indiana Jones, Dr. Spock, Batman, and others) reflect America's tastes and values? Do "survivor TV" shows reflect the popular taste for a new kind of hero/heroine?

2. What images do you personally associate with the phrase "romantic love"?

3. Which men and women of your own time come closest to fulfilling nineteenth-century conceptions of the romantic hero? How so?

4. The "Byronic personality" is usually configured as one who leads an extraordinary life style and experiences an operatic demise. Has contemporary culture produced any individuals who fit this description? Cite names and defend your choices.

Chapter 29: The Romantic Style in Art and Music

I. CHAPTER OBJECTIVE:

To explore the basic features of the romantic style in the arts of the nineteenth century

AM I FAMILIAR WITH:

- the basic characteristics of the romantic style in art and music?
- the principal exponents of heroic and nationalistic themes in the visual arts: Gros, Géricault, Goya, Delacroix, Bartholdi, Rude?
- the major trends in nineteenth-century architecture?
- the role of nationalism in the arts?
- the principal exponents of the romantic style in music: Beethoven, Schubert, Berlioz, Chopin?
- the significance of romantic dance and opera?

II. OUTLINE

A. The Romantic Style

B. Romantic Themes

    1. heroism

    2. nationalism

C. Romantic Artists

    1. painting: Gros, Goya, Géricault, Delacroix

    2. sculpture: Bartholdi, Rude, Lewis, Cordier

D. Trends in Nineteenth-Century Architecture

    1. neomedievalism

    2. exoticism in Western architecture

E. The Romantic Style in Music

    1. instrumental and vocal composition

        a. Beethoven

        b. German art songs: Schubert

        c. Berlioz

        d. Chopin

    2. ballet

    3. romantic opera

        a. Verdi

        b. Wagner

III. KEY TERMS: CAN I DEFINE/EXPLAIN?

(What? Why important?)

heroic allegory

neomedievalism

nationalism

aquatint

arabesque

lied [LEED]

romantic symphony

opus

virtuoso [ver CHEW oh so]

music-drama

leitmotif [LEYET moh teef]

idée-fixe [ee DAY FEEKS]

arpeggio [ahr PEJ ee oh]

étude [ay TOOD]

impromptu [im PROM too]

nocturne

program music

prima ballerina [PREE ma]

scherzo [SKER tsow]

tremolo [TREM a low]

dynamics (music)

IV. KEY NAMES: CAN I IDENTIFY?

(Who? What? When? Where?)

Gros [GROW]

Géricault [zhe ree KOW]

Goya

Disasters of War

Delacroix

Bartholdi [bar THOL dee]

Rude [ROOD]

Lewis

Cordier [cor dee AY]

Royal Pavilion

Nash

Saint Patrick's Cathedral

Beethoven

Schubert [SHOO berh]

Erlking

Berlioz [ber lee OWZ]

Symphonie fantastique [SAM foh nee fan tahs TEEK]

Chopin [show PAN]

Garnier [gahr nee AY]

Taglioni [tal YOW nay]

Tchaikovsky [cheye KAHF skee]

Verdi [VEHR dee]

Wagner [VAHG nur]

V. KEY DATES

- 1799 = Beethoven dedicates Symphony No. 3 to Napoleon
- 1808 = Napoleon's troops occupy Madrid
- 1830 = Revolution of 1830 (France); Maria Taglioni makes her London debut
- 1851 = Great Exhibition of London
- 1874 = Wagner completes *The Ring*
- 1884 = Bartholdi sends the Statue of Liberty to America

VI. VOCABULARY BUILDING: CAN I DEFINE?

austerity

malevolence

frigate

macabre

augment

ethnological

VII. SAMPLE MULTIPLE CHOICE QUESTIONS

1. NOT true of the heroic themes in the art of Géricault, Goya, and Delacroix:

   a. they often involve violent action

   b. they feature victims of nature and war

   c. they are based in religion, myth, or fantasy

   d. they emphasize the immediacy of the event

2. In Delacroix's *Liberty Leading the People,* the "people" include all except

   a. the aristocracy.

   b. the middle class.

   c. the lower class.

   d. racial minorities.

3. Cordier's *African* and Nash's *Royal Pavilion* were expressions of nineteenth-century

   a. medievalism.

   b. exoticism.

   c. nationalism.

   d. all of these.

4. Of nineteenth-century music it is true to say that

   a. the orchestra grew to grand proportions.

   b. classical composition was entirely abandoned.

   c. most music was composed for the human voice.

   d. program music was totally avoided.

5. The name Taglioni is associated with

   a. sculpture.

   b. ballet.

   c. architecture.

   d. music.

(Answers appear on page x.)

VIII. ESSAY QUESTIONS/WRITING EXERCISE

1. Describe the historical background for each of the following, explaining the "heroic" historical events that inspired each: *The Third of May, 1808; The Raft of the Medusa; Liberty Leading the People.*

2. What musical forms dominated the romantic style in music? How did romantic music differ from that of the classical era? (Listen to the compositions discussed in this chapter, Music Listening Selections II-12, 13, 14, 15, as a basis for your essay and compare them with those that accompany chapter 26, MLS 9 and 10.)

3. Which particular literary themes (see chapters 27 and 28) were especially favored by the painters and composers of the romantic era? Why so?

4. Discuss the role played by nationalism in the art, architecture, and music of the romantic era.

5. Why is ballet considered a "romantic" art form? Might this kind of dance also be regarded as "classical"? How so?

IX. MAKING CONNECTIONS

1. Listen to a Mozart symphony, then to a Beethoven Symphony. Describe the differences in "affect," that is, the feelings or emotions evoked by each listening experience.

2. Choose a piece of art or music from your own day and time that, in your view, conveys the romantic sensibility and a second one that pursues a heroic theme.

3. Describe a theatrical or cinematic work of the last two decades that romanticizes a historical event (e.g., *Dances with Wolves, Malcolm X, Apollo 13, Saving Private Ryan, The Patriot*). What features (characterization, background music, setting, etc.) contributed to shaping a romantic image?

4. Can you describe any visual or aural experience from your childhood years that you have romanticized as you grew older? How does memory work to romanticize experience?

X. SYNTHESIS PART I: THE ROMANTIC ERA

Write an extended essay on any ONE of the following:

1. Compare the romantic and neoclassical styles (chapter 26) as two expressions of the nineteenth century. Be sure to cite specific examples.

2. Choose any one of the following as a subject for an essay on the Romantic Era. Cite specific examples from art, music, and literature that support your points of view.

    (a) individualism and heroism

    (b) nature and the physical world

    (c) woman as subject, theme, creator

3. Evaluate the relative impact of each of the following on the romantic sensibility: (a) Enlightenment rationalism, (b) industrialism, (c) nationalism, and (d) Darwin's theories.

XI. BONUS

Franz Schubert (1797–1828)

Erlkönig (The Erlking)

Narrator

Wer reitet so spät durch Nacht und Wind?	Who rides so late through the night and the wind?
Es ist der Vater mit seinem Kind;	It is the father with his child;
Er hat den Knaben wohl in dem Arm,	he holds the boy close in his arms,
Er fasst ihn sicher, er hält ihn warm.	he clutches him securely, he holds him warmly.

Father

"Mein Sohn, was birgst du so bang dein Gesicht?"	"My son, why do you hide your face so anxiously?"

Son

"Siehst, Vater, du den Erlkönig nicht?	"Father, don't you see the Erlking?
Den Erlenkönig mit Kron' und Schweif?"	The Erlking with his crown and train?"

Father

"Mein Sohn, es ist ein Nebelstreif."	"My son, it is a streak of mist."

Erlking

"Du liebes Kind, komm, geh mit mir!	"Dear child, come, go with me!
Gar schöne Spiele spiel' ich mit dir,	I'll play the prettiest games with you.
Manch bunte Blumen sind an dem Strand,	Many colored flowers grow along the shore;
Meine Mutter hat manch gülden Gewand."	My mother has many golden garments."

Son

"Mein Vater, mein Vater, und hörest du nicht,	"My father, my father, and don't you hear
Was Erlenkönig mir leise verspricht?"	the Erlking whispering promises to me?"

Father

"Sei ruhig, bleibe ruhig, mein kind:	Be quiet, stay quiet, my child;
In dürren Blättern säuselt der Wind"	the wind is rustling in the dead leaves."

Erlking

"Willst, feiner Knabe, du mit mir gehn?	"My handsome boy will you come with me?
Meine Töchter sollen dich warten schön;	My daughters shall wait upon you;
Mein Töchter führen den nächtlichen Reihn	my daughters lead off in the dance every night,
Und weigen und tanzen und singen dich ein."	and cradle and dance and sing you to sleep."

Son

"Mein Vater, mein Vater, und siehst du nicht dort.	"My father, my father, and don't you see there
Erlkönigs Töcher am düstern Ort?"	the Erlking's daughters in the shadows?"

Father

"Mein Sohn, mein sohn, ich seh' es genau:	"My son, my son, I see it clearly;
Es scheinen die alten Weiden so grau."	the old willows look so gray."

Erlking

"Ich liebe dich, mich reizt deine schöne Gestalt;	"I love you, your beautiful figure delights me!
Und bist du nicht willig, so brauch' ich Gewalt."	And if you are not willing, then I shall use force!"

Son

"Mein Vater, mein Vater, jetzt fasst er mich an!	"My father, my father, now he is taking hold of me!
Erlkönig hat mir ein Leids getan!"	The Erlking has hurt me!"

Narrator

Dem Vater grauset's, er reitet geschwind,	The father shudders, he rides swiftly on;
Er hält in Armen das ächzende Kind,	he holds in his arms the moaning child,
Erreicht den Hof mit Muhe und Not;	he reaches the courtyard weary and anxious:
In seinen Armem das Kind war tot.	in his arms the child was dead.

TYPICAL SEATING ARRANGEMENTS FOR ORCHESTRA AND BAND

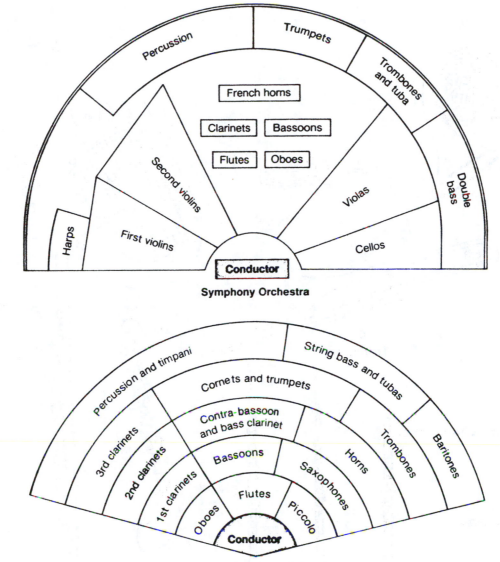

Symphony Orchestra

Concert (Symphonic) Band

From Brown & Benchmark, Humanities Transparencies, 2d ed.
Copyright © 1991 Times Mirror Higher Education Group, Inc., Dubuque, Iowa.
All Right Reserved. Reprinted by permission.

BRASS AND WOODWIND INSTRUMENTS

Brass

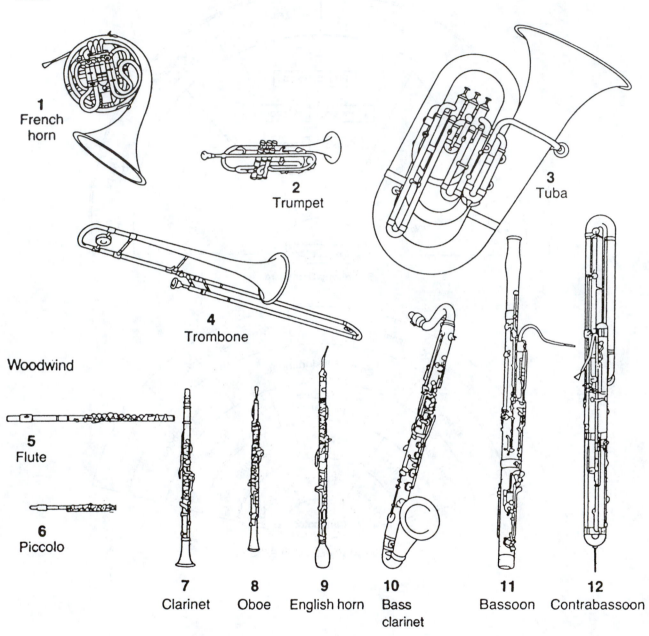

1
French
horn

2
Trumpet

3
Tuba

4
Trombone

Woodwind

5
Flute

6
Piccolo

7
Clarinet

8
Oboe

9
English horn

10
Bass
clarinet

11
Bassoon

12
Contrabassoon

STRING INSTRUMENTS

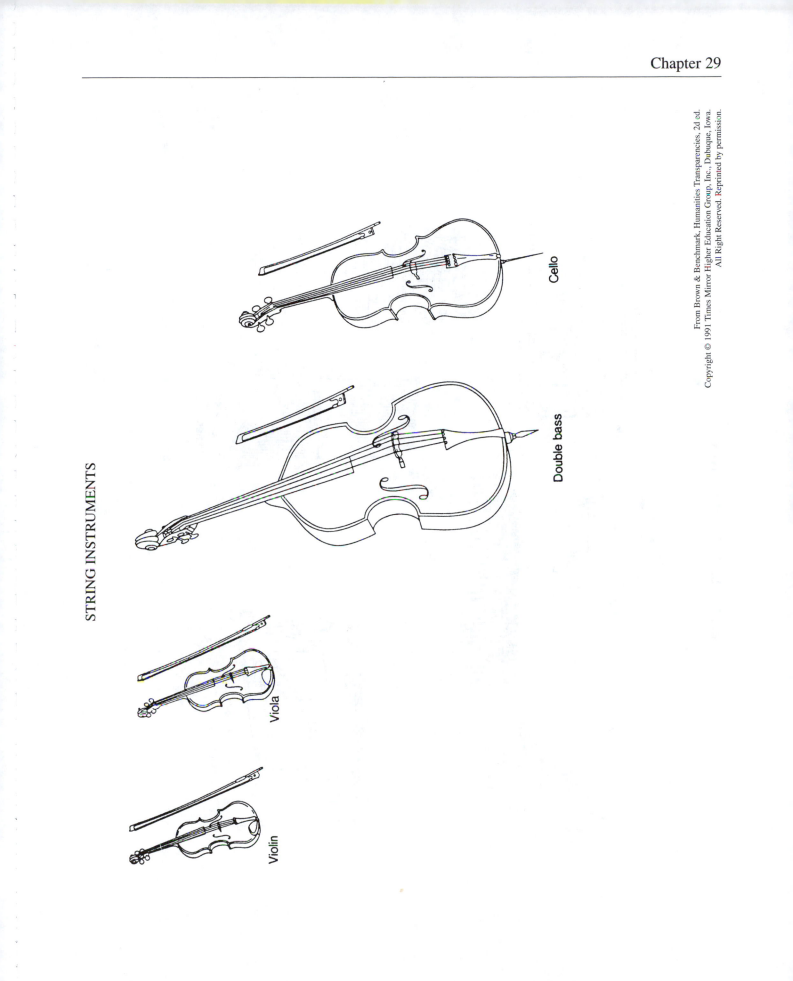

Cello

Double bass

Viola

Violin

PERCUSSION INSTRUMENTS

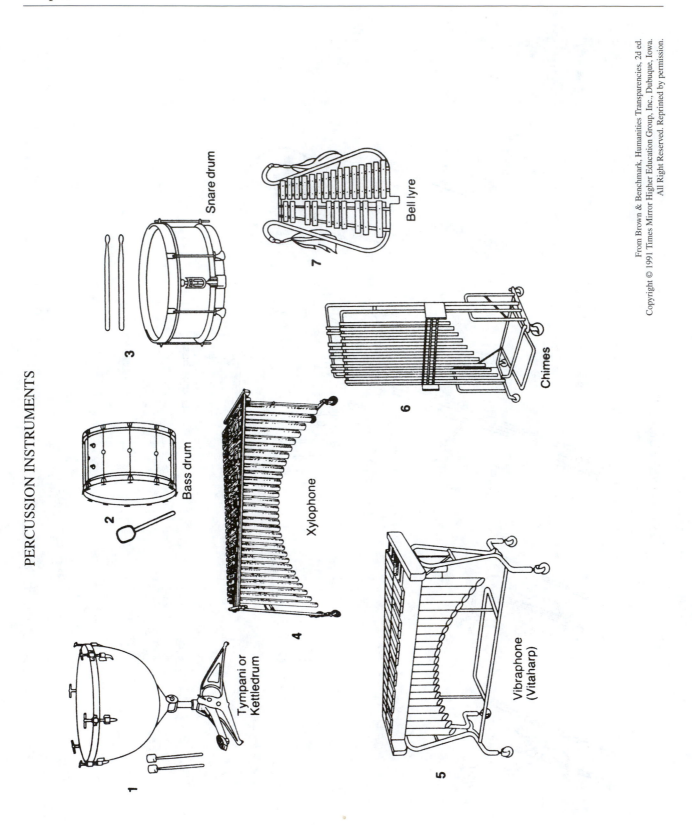

1 Tympani or Kettledrum

2 Bass drum

3 Snare drum

4 Xylophone

5 Vibraphone (Vitaharp)

6 Chimes

7 Bell lyre

PART II: REALISM AND THE MODERNIST TURN

Chapter 30: Industry, Empire, and the Realist Style

I. CHAPTER OBJECTIVE:

To examine mid-nineteenth-century realism in a global historical context

AM I FAMILIAR WITH:

- the factors that contributed to Western global dominion: industrialism, colonialism, nationalism, imperialism?
- the social theories of Mill and Marx?
- the shift from romanticism to realism in literature, the visual arts, music?
- technologies as vehicles of realism: journalism, photography, lithography?

II. OUTLINE

A. The Historical Context

1. advancing industrialism
2. colonialism and modern imperialism
3. China and the West
4. social and economic realities

B. Social Theory

1. conservatism; liberalism; utilitarianism; socialism
2. Marx and Engels
3. Mill and women's rights

C. Realism in Literature

1. Dickens and Twain
2. Dostoevsky and Tolstoy
3. Flaubert and Kate Chopin
4. Ibsen and realist drama

D. Realism in the Visual Arts

1. the birth of photography
2. Courbet
3. Daumier
4. Manet
5. American realist painting

E. Late Nineteenth-Century Architecture

    1. cast iron: Paxton and Eiffel

    2. Sullivan and the skyscraper

F. Realism in Music

III. KEY TERMS: CAN I DEFINE/EXPLAIN?

(What? Why important?)

industrialism

colonialism

"the white man's burden"

opium wars

capitalism

conservatism

liberalism

utilitarianism

socialism

communism

bourgeoisie [boor zhwah ZEE]

proletariat realism

"new historicism"

lithography [li THOG rah fee]

daguerreotype [da GEHR ow teyep]

chattel slavery

naturalism

verismo [vehr RIZ mow]

IV. KEY NAMES: CAN I IDENTIFY?

(Who? What? When? Where?)

Kipling

Lin Zexu [lin see zhoo]

Queen Victoria

Bentham

Mill

Proudhon [proo DOHN]

Marx

Engels

Seneca Falls

Dickens

Twain

Dostoevsky [dahs toy EV skee]

Tolstoy

Repin

Flaubert [flow BEHR]

Kate Chopin [SHOW pan]

Ibsen

Talbot

Daguerre [dah GEHR]

Brady

Cameron

Courbet [coor BAY]

Millet [mee LAY]

Daumier [dow mee AY]

Nadar [NAY dahr]

Manet [ma NAY]

Salon des Refusés [sah LON day reh foo ZAY]

Harnett

Eakins

Homer

Tanner

Paxton

Crystal Palace

Eiffel [eye FEL]

Sullivan

Puccini [poo CHEE nee]

V. KEY DATES

- 1839 = Daguerre's first photographic experiments
- 1839-1842 = Opium Wars
- 1848 = *Communist Manifesto* completed; American feminists meet at Seneca Falls, N.Y.
- 1853 = Japan forced to open its doors to Western trade

- 1856 = structural steel perfected
- 1857 = Flaubert's *Madame Bovary* published
- 1863 = *Salon des Refusés* (Salon of the Rejected Artists)

VI. VOCABULARY BUILDING: CAN I DEFINE?

opium

entrepreneur

plebeian

vernacular

nouveau riche [noo vow REESH]

courtesan

impending

dispassionate

VII. SAMPLE MULTIPLE CHOICE QUESTIONS

1. John Stuart Mill argued that, traditionally, men have wanted women to be

   a. no different than slaves.

   b. independent-minded.

   c. devoted to submission and meekness.

   d. mischievous and daring.

2. The new historicists brought critical and controversial study to the field of

   a. women's rights.

   b. religious history.

   c. class struggle.

   d. early societies.

3. In the *Communist Manifesto* Marx and Engels envision as the new ruling class

   a. the proletariat.

   b. the bourgeoisie.

   c. the *nouveau riche.*

   d. the entrepreneurs.

4. In Ibsen's *Doll's House,* Nora leaves Torvald because

   a. she is tired of taking care of the children.

   b. she has found another lover.

   c. she has lost confidence in his ability to support her.

   d. she wishes to stand alone and make her own decisions.

5. The artist who said "Show me an angel and I'll paint one" was

   a. Manet.

   b. Courbet.

   c. Daumier.

   d. Homer.

6. The social realist Daumier

   a. satirized modern technology.

   b. was jailed for criticizing the government.

   c. pioneered the art of lithography.

   d. all of the above.

(Answers appear on page x.)

VIII. VISUAL/SPATIAL EXERCISE

In the GRAPHIC CLUSTER on the next page, write freely to explore ideas and relationships between the names and styles identified in the "windows."

VARIETIES OF REALISM

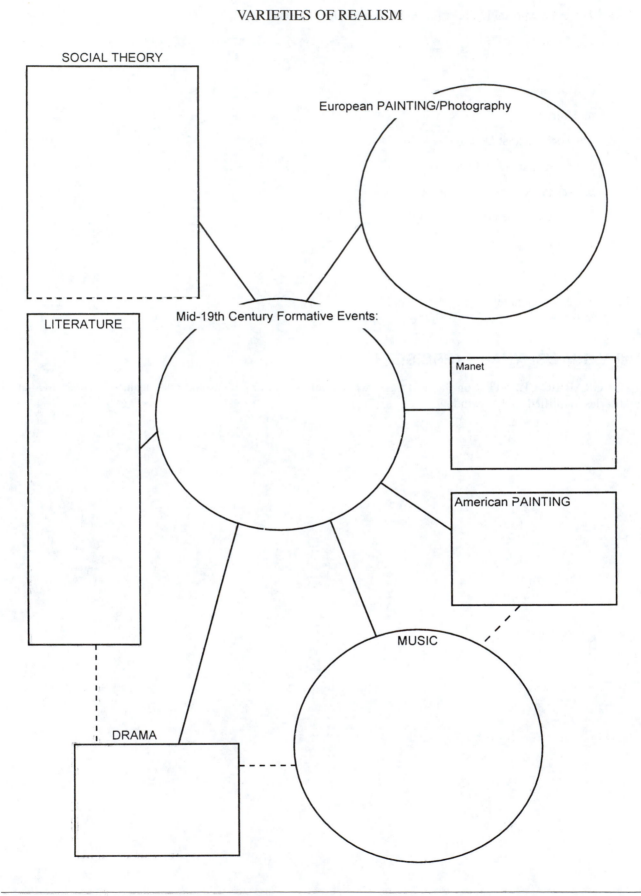

SOCIAL THEORY

European PAINTING/Photography

LITERATURE

Mid-19th Century Formative Events:

Manet

American PAINTING

MUSIC

DRAMA

IX. ESSAY QUESTIONS/WRITING EXERCISE

1. Discuss any three of the following from the point of view of scandal and/or innovation; how did each overturn traditional views? How does each represent the shift to realism?

   (a) Courbet's *The Stone Breakers*

   (b) Dickens' *Old Curiosity Shop*

   (c) Twain's *Huckleberry Finn*

   (d) Manet's *Déjeuner sur l'herbe*

   (e) Puccini's *Madame Butterfly*

2. Examine the role of the nineteenth-century female as perceived by any three of the following: Mill, Flaubert, Ibsen, Kate Chopin, and Manet.

3. How did journalism, lithography, and photography serve nineteenth-century society in its quest for greater realism? Cite specific examples.

4. Discuss realism as a typically American style. Include in your essay an evaluation of the realist features in the writings of Twain and Kate Chopin and in the paintings of Harnett, Homer, Tanner, and Eakins.

5. How did industrialism and urban expansion affect the arts of the late nineteenth century?

X. MAKING CONNECTIONS

1. Do today's sophisticated technologies contribute to realism in the arts, as they seem to have done in the nineteenth century? Why or why not?

2. Viewers of Manet's *Déjeuner* initially responded to its public display by attacking the canvas with their umbrellas. What kind of art might evoke (or has evoked) a comparable response in our own time?

3. Compare Puccini's *Madama Butterfly* with the popular musical drama, *Miss Saigon*. Which evokes the greater affective response? Why?

4. How does the satiric realism of Twain's *Huckleberry Finn* compare with that of other great literary satires, such as Voltaire's *Candide* (see chapter 25)?

XI. BONUS

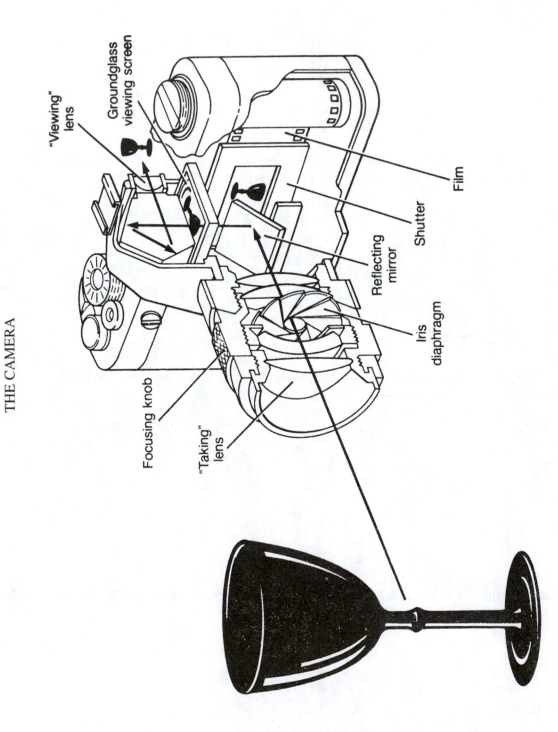

THE CAMERA

"Viewing" lens

Groundglass viewing screen

Focusing knob

"Taking" lens

Reflecting mirror

Iris diaphragm

Shutter

Film

Chapter 31: The Move Toward Modernism

I. CHAPTER OBJECTIVE:

To examine the principal cultural and artistic movements of the late nineteenth century

AM I FAMILIAR WITH:

- the impact of science and technology on late nineteenth-century culture?
- the major figures of late nineteenth-century philosophy and literature?
- symbolism and impressionism as style in the arts of the West?
- the influence of non-Western cultures (Oceania, Africa, and Japan) on Western art and design?
- how postimpressionism reflects the art-for-art's sake spirit?

II. OUTLINE

  A. The Historical Context for the Late Nineteenth Century

      1. Paris as cultural mecca

      2. scientific and technological developments

  B. Philosophy and Literature

      1. Nietzsche

      2. Bergson

      3. Symbolism: Mallarmé

  C. Symbolism in the Arts

  D. Impressionism

      1. Music: Debussy

      2. Painting: Monet, Renoir, Pissarro, Degas

  E. The Arts at the End of the Century

      1. the influence of Japanese art

      2. art nouveau

      3. sculpture

          a. Degas

          b. Rodin

      4. dance

  F. The Arts of Africa and Oceania

  G. Postimpressionism

      1. van Gogh

      2. Gauguin

3. Seurat

4. Cézanne

III. KEY TERMS: CAN I DEFINE/EXPLAIN?

(What? Why important?)

materialism

"slave morality"

Übermensch [OO ber manch]

intuition

duration

symbolism

impressionism

primitivism

woodblock/woodcut

"slice of life"

art nouveau [AHR noo VOW]

tonic ("home tone")

ukiyo [yoo KEE yoh]

bird's eye view

japonisme

cloisonné [clwah son NAY]

pointillism

postimpressionism

art for art's sake

IV. KEY NAMES: CAN I IDENTIFY?

(Who? What? When? Where?)

Edison

Nietzsche [NEET che]

Bergson [berg SOWN]

Mallarmé [mal ahr MAY]

Debussy [deb yoo SEE]

Nijinsky [ni ZHIN skee]

Helmholtz

Chevreul [shv ROOL]

Hodler [HOWD lar]

Monet [mow NAY]

Rouen [roo AHN]

Pissarro [pi SAHR oh]

Renoir [ren WAHR]

Degas [de GAH]

Muybridge [MEYE brig]

Hokusai [how koo SEYE]

Cassatt [ke SAHT]

Morisot [mow ree SOW]

Toulouse-Lautrec [too LOOZ low TREK]

Rodin [row DAN]

Duncan

Oceania

Maori [may YU ree]

Yoruba

Mali

King Gele

van Gogh [fon GOH]

Gauguin [gow GAN]

Noa Noa

Seurat [se RAHT]

Grand Jatte [grand JAHT]

Cézanne [say ZAHN]

Mont Sainte-Victoire [mon san ve TWAR]

V. KEY DATES

- 1873 = Maxwell publishes *Treatise on Electricity and Magnetism;* Monet paints *Impression: Sunrise*
- 1875 = A.G. Bell invents telephone
- 1877 = Edison invents the phonograph
- 1879 = Edison perfects incandescent light bulb
- 1885 = Benz develops gasoline-powered motor car
- 1880-1886 = Seurat paints *La Grand Jatte*
- 1891 = Edison and Dickson patent first American motion picture system

VI. VOCABULARY BUILDING: CAN I DEFINE?

aphorism

caustic

demimonde

abstract

iconoclasm

VII. SAMPLE MULTIPLE CHOICE QUESTIONS

1. The philosopher who was most concerned with exploring the shifting and elusive perception of time was

    a. Nietzsche.

    b. Bergson.

    c. Mallarmé.

    d. Hodler.

2. His effort to "redo nature after Poussin"

    a. led Cézanne to seek simplified, enduring forms.

    b. prompted Toulouse-Lautrec to return to academic art.

    c. led Monet to renounce black as a color.

    d. resulted in Gauguin's search for exotic landscape.

3. The music of Debussy did NOT

    a. deviate from the traditional practice of returning harmonies to the tonic.

    b. reveal a fascination with tone color.

    c. imitate the clarity of the classical sonata form.

    d. employ shifting harmonies and nebulous effects.

4. The subject matter of the impressionist painters included all EXCEPT

    a. street scenes.

    b. landscapes.

    c. cafe life.

    d. religious themes.

5. The work of the photographer Eadweard Muybridge had a major impact on the art of

    a. Renoir.

    b. Degas.

    c. Gauguin.

    d. Seurat.

(Answers appear on page x.)

VIII. ESSAY QUESTIONS/WRITING EXERCISE

1. Define each of the following styles and describe the proponents of each in the arts of the late nineteenth century: symbolism; impressionism; art nouveau, postimpressionism.

2. Nietzsche asks: "Is not the nineteenth century, especially at its close, . . . a century of *decadence?*" Do you agree with this assessment? If so, why? If not, why?

3. In what ways did the postimpressionist painters break with impressionism? What interests did they share? Cite specific examples to illustrate your point of view.

4. What were the principal artistic achievements of nineteenth-century Japan, Africa, and Oceania? How did the West respond to these forms of non-European art?

5. What parallels might be drawn between the music, sculpture, and dance of the late nineteenth century? Cite specific examples.

IX. MAKING CONNECTIONS

1. In the late nineteenth century, Africa, Japan, and Polynesia were considered exotic lands. What places or things are considered "exotic" today? Does today's view of the exotic influence the arts? How so?

2. Why, in your view, has Vincent van Gogh become such a "culture hero" in our own time?

3. If you have attended live (or watched video) performances of both classical ballet and modern dance, discuss the differences between the two. Which do you prefer? Why?

4. In the poem "Afternoon of a Faun" images are intimately linked to the world of the senses. Find three other works of art (or music) in this chapter of which the same might be said.

X. SYNTHESIS PART II: THE MODERNIST TURN

Write an extended essay on any ONE of the following:

1. In what ways might each of the following figures be called "the last of the romantics"? In what ways might they be called the pioneers of modernism?

Marx	Nietzsche
Ibsen	Debussy
Mallarmé	Monet

2. Describe in your own words the major features of the so-called "modernist turn" that occurred in the late nineteenth century. What features in philosophy, literature, and the arts strongly suggest a new direction? Be sure to cite examples.

3. Discuss the various ways in which changing technology affected the arts of the late nineteenth century. Cite specific examples.

4. Discuss the roles of the church, the court, and the middle-class entrepreneur as patrons of the arts during the nineteenth century? How did these circumstances compare with earlier centuries you have studied?

5. Which of the impressionist and postimpressionist paintings are your favorites? Why? Which tell you most about the culture of the late nineteenth century?

BOOK 6
MODERNISM, GLOBALISM, AND THE INFORMATION AGE

PART I: THE TRIUMPH OF MODERNISM

Chapter 32: The Modernist Assault

I. CHAPTER OBJECTIVE:

To evaluate antitraditionalism in the arts in the early twentieth century

AM I FAMILIAR WITH:

- the impact of technology and the new physics on the arts?
- the imagist movement in early twentieth-century poetry?
- the major styles in modern art and architecture: cubism, futurism, fauvism, nonobjective art, the international style?
- antitraditional forms of expression in music and dance?
- the role of film as an early modern phenomenon?

II. OUTLINE

A. Historical Context

1. the global village

2. the new physics

B. Early Twentieth-Century Poetry

1. imagists

2. Frost

C. Early Twentieth-Century Visual Art

1. cubism

2. futurism

3. the birth of film

4. fauvism

5. abstract sculpture

6. nonobjective art

7. constructivism

    D. Early Twentieth-Century Architecture

       1. Wright

       2. the Bauhaus

       3. Le Corbusier

    E. Early Twentieth-Century Music and Dance

       1. Schoenberg

       2. Stravinsky

       3. dance

III. KEY TERMS: CAN I DEFINE/EXPLAIN?

(What? Why important?)

quanta

relativity

principle of uncertainty

avant-garde [ah vahnt GARD]

imagist

abstraction

haiku [heye KOO]

analytic cubism

synthetic cubism

collage

futurism

fauvism

nonobjective art

international style

cantilever

ferroconcrete

suprematism

constructivism

theosophy

pilotis [pi LOH tis]

atonality

polytonality

polyrhythm

serial technique

twelve-tone system

IV. KEY NAMES: CAN I IDENTIFY?

(Who? What? When? Where?)

Planck

Einstein

Heisenberg

Pound

Frost

Picasso

Braque [BRAHK]

Archipenko

Marinetti

Balla

Boccioni [bow CHOW nee]

Matisse

Duchamp [doo SHAHM]

Armory Show

Brancusi

Weston

Kandinsky

Mondrian [mown dree AHN]

De Stijl [de STEYEL]

Rietvelt [REET felt]

Malevich [MAL ev itch]

Popova [POP ow vah]

Porter

Griffith

Wright

Bauhaus [BAHW hahws]

Gropius

Le Corbusier [le kowr boo ZEEAY]

Schoenberg [SHURN berg]

Stravinsky

Ballet Russes [bah LAY ROOS]

Nijinsky [ni ZHIN skee]

Graham

V. KEY DATES

- 1900 = Planck introduces quantum physics
- 1900-1905 = first silent films
- 1905 = Einstein issues his special theory of relativity; first *fauve* exhibition in Paris
- 1907 = Picasso completes *Les Demoiselles d'Avignon*
- 1913 = Debut performance of Stravinsky's *Rite of Spring*
- 1919 = Gropius founds the Bauhaus in Weimar
- 1920 = Heisenberg posits the principle of uncertainty

VI. VOCABULARY BUILDING: CAN I DEFINE?

dissipate

disjunctive

allusion

quintessential

chromatic

dissonance

VII. SAMPLE MULTIPLE CHOICE QUESTIONS

1. In their poems, the imagist poets tried to achieve
   a. a new lyricism and strong sentiment.
   b. a pared down, abstract style.
   c. the revival of fixed meter.
   d. a consistent use of rhyme.

2. The movement known as *De Stijl* is associated with the name
   a. Picasso.
   b. Boccioni.
   c. Mondrian.
   d. Kandinsky.

3. A major element in the shift from analytic to synthetic cubism was

   a. the use of collage.

   b. a move toward nonobjectivity.

   c. the elimination of all color.

   d. an effort to capture motion on canvas.

4. The names Gropius and Le Corbusier are associated with the

   a. birth of motion pictures.

   b. first efforts at abstract sculpture.

   c. international style in architecture.

   d. twelve-tone system in music.

5. The arts of the early twentieth century reflect ALL EXCEPT the

   a. disjunctive juxtaposition of motifs.

   b. influence of new theories of time and space.

   c. confidence in an orderly cosmos.

   d. search for the essential qualities of the subject.

(Answers appear on page xi.)

VIII. VISUAL/SPATIAL EXERCISE

Using the GRAPHIC CLUSTER on the next page, write freely to explore associations between styles and movements. You may write within or across the "windows" in the cluster.

THE MODERNIST ASSAULT ON TRADITION

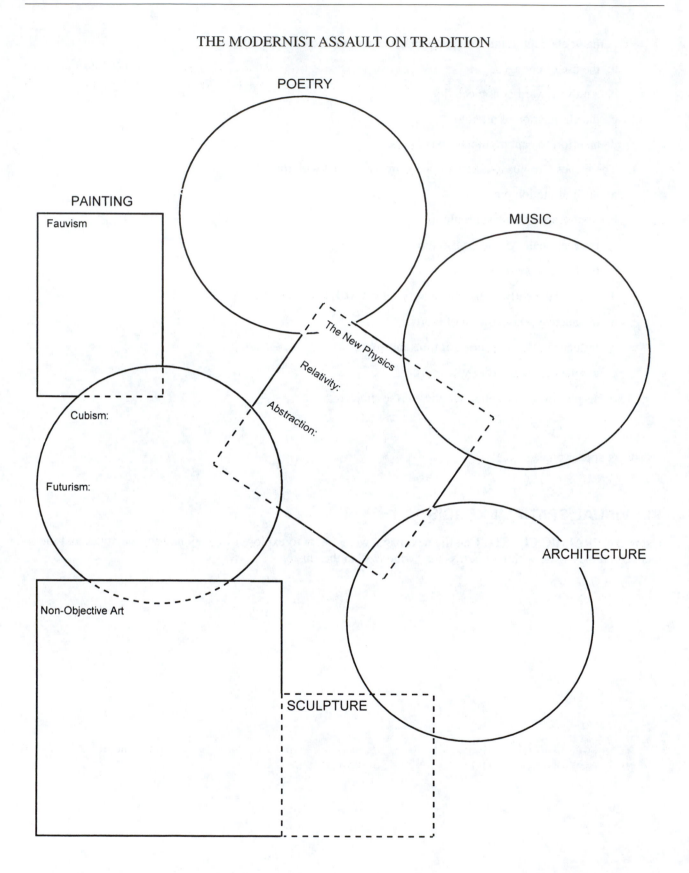

POETRY

PAINTING

Fauvism

MUSIC

The New Physics

Relativity:

Abstraction:

Cubism:

Futurism:

ARCHITECTURE

Non-Objective Art

SCULPTURE

IX. ESSAY QUESTIONS/WRITING EXERCISE

1. Use the sentences: "make it new," "I took the road less traveled by," and "[we must] free art from the burden of the Object" in an essay that describes the spirit of early modernism. Be sure to identify the source of each phrase, and cite visual examples from the chapter wherever appropriate.

2. What is nonobjective art? Describe the differences between the styles of the following artists: Kandinsky, Mondrian, Malevich, Brancusi.

3. What radical features did Schoenberg and Stravinsky introduce into early twentieth-century music? (Suggested Music Listening Selections II-17 and 18.)

4. Compare Picasso's *Demoiselles d'Avignon* and Stravinsky's *Rite of Spring:* what were the public's initial reactions to each? What was each artist trying to achieve? Finally, what does each tell us about the early twentieth century?

5. FILMS FOR THIS CHAPTER: *A Trip to the Moon; The Great Train Robbery.* See either one of the films and write a brief essay on how and what it reflects of the key ideas and themes of this chapter.

X. MAKING CONNECTIONS

1. Compose a nonobjective crayon or painted composition whose elements (lines, shapes, colors) have *personal* meaning for you. Give the composition a title. OR write an imagist poem using elements that have *personal* meaning; then put the poem into everyday language.

2. In 1905, the audience hissed and booed the debut performance of Stravinsky's *Rite of Spring*. What kind of music might evoke a comparable response today. Why so?

3. Locate a building or home in your area that is indebted to the architectural innovations of either Frank Lloyd Wright, Walter Gropius, or Le Corbusier. Describe.

4. Make a short film or video that employs the principles of abstraction and disjunction evidenced in early modern art.

Chapter 33: The Freudian Revolution

I. CHAPTER OBJECTIVE:

To examine the impact of Sigmund Freud and the new psychology on the arts of the twentieth century

AM I FAMILIAR WITH:

- the basic theories of Freud and Freudian psychoanalysis?
- the impact of the new psychology on literature: Proust, Kafka, Joyce, e.e. cummings?
- how the new psychology influenced the birth of key movements in the arts: expressionism, dada, and surrealism?

II. OUTLINE

A. The Freudian Revolution

   1. Freud's theories and techniques

   2. Freud's model of the psyche

   3. Jung's archetypal subconscious

B. Impact of the New Psychology on Literature

   1. Proust

   2. Kafka

   3. Joyce

   4. e.e. cummings

C. Impact of the New Psychology on the Arts

   1. expressionism

     a. Munch

     b. Kirchner

   2. metaphysical art and fantasy

     a. de Chirico

     b. Chagall

   3. dadaism

   4. surrealism

     a. Picasso, Miro, and Klee

     b. Magritte and Dali

     c. O'Keeffe and Kahlo

   5. photography and film

6. early twentieth-century music

    a. Strauss

    b. Schoenberg

III. KEY TERMS: CAN I DEFINE/EXPLAIN?

(What? Why important?)

psyche [SEYE kee]

subconscious

psychoanalysis

id/ego/superego

libido [li BEE dow]

collective unconscious

archetype [AHR ki teyep]

stream of consciousness

interior monologue

free association

improvisation

concrete poetry

metaphysical art

theater of cruelty

expressionism

dadaism

surrealism

magic realism

ready-made sculpture

"found object"

method acting

photomontage [FOW tow mahn tazh]

monodrama

Sprechtstimme [SHPREK shti mu]

IV. KEY NAMES: CAN I IDENTIFY?

(Who? What? When? Where?)

Freud

Adler

Jung [YOONG]

Proust [PROOST]

Kafka

Joyce

Apollinaire

cummings

Munch [MOONK]

Kirchner [KIRK ner]

de Chirico [de KI ree kow]

Chagall

Miro [mee ROW]

Klee [CLAY]

Breton [breh TON]

Surrealist Manifesto

Fountain

Magritte [mah GREET]

Dali

O'Keeffe

Kahlo [KAH low]

Höch [HOWK]

Oppenheim

Satie [sah TEE]

Pierrot Lunaire [PEE ah row LOO nayr]

V. KEY DATES

- 1900 = Freud publishes *The Interpretation of Dreams*
- 1912 = Schoenberg composes *Pierrot Lunaire*
- 1913 = Freud publishes *Totem and Taboo*
- 1916 = "dada" founded in Zurich
- 1922 = Joyce publishes *Ulysses*
- 1924 = Breton writes the first Surrealist Manifesto
- 1930 = Freud publishes *Civilization and Its Discontents*

VI. VOCABULARY BUILDING: CAN I DEFINE?

puberty

sublimation

voyeur

primal

nihilism

desiccated

VII. SAMPLE MULTIPLE CHOICE QUESTIONS

1. Freud theorized that human instinct was driven by

    a. sex.

    b. love.

    c. fear.

    d. hate.

2. In *Civilization and Its Discontents,* Freud says that religion

    a. is a political tool to control mass opinion.

    b. is humankind's only hope for happiness.

    c. must be classed among humankind's mass delusions.

    d. serves efficiently to temper human aggression.

3. Jung described the collective unconscious as

    a. synonymous with Freud's ego.

    b. responsible for the wars between the sexes.

    c. manifested in myths, fairytales, and dreams.

    d. all of the above.

4. The object that triggers the recollection of the past for Proust was a

    a. spoonful of tea.

    b. a taste of cake.

    c. a sexual encounter.

    d. the first snowfall.

5. The surrealist movement was devoted to making art that

    a. freed itself of rational control.

    b. used brightly colored forms in equilibrium.

    c. paid homage to the new machine age.

    d. drew directly on photographic sources.

(Answers appear on page xi.)

VIII. VISUAL/SPATIAL EXERCISE

Surrealist Exercise: Using ONE of the following techniques, describe your emotional responses to your last telephone conversation or to some recent troubling event:

(1) stream of consciousness

(2) concrete poetry: a poem in the shape of an external object

(3) collage assembled according to the laws of chance

IX. ESSAY QUESTIONS/WRITING EXERCISE

1. In your view, which one of the literary selections in this chapter best reflects the mechanics of the psyche as described by Sigmund Freud? Explain how and why it does so.

2. What were the aims of the surrealists, as defined by Breton in the Surrealist Manifesto? In your view, which of the artists represented in this chapter best fulfills the surrealist mission? How so?

3. In what ways were the writings of Freud "revolutionary"? In what ways has Freud's influence reached beyond the literature, art, and music of the early twentieth century? Has this influence persisted into contemporary art?

4. Why and how does music that is written for film often "work" better in a cinematic context? Find examples from films that illustrate this phenomenon.

5. FILMS FOR THIS CHAPTER: *Un chien Andalou; Le Sang d'un Poete; La Belle et la Bête.* See any one of these films and write a brief essay on how the film reflects the ideas and themes presented in this chapter.

X. MAKING CONNECTIONS

1. From any current magazine, select an advertisement that reflects the influence of Surrealism. To which of the surrealists does it owe the most?

2. Compare a Kafka short story with an Alfred Hitchcock film. What devices does each employ to create situations of suspense, ambiguity, and apprehension?

3. Recount in some detail a recent or recurrent dream that might serve as the subject of a surrealist painting, story, or drama.

4. Experiment with "psychic automatism" by making a drawing out of the "doodles" you produce while talking on the telephone or while listening to music. How does the final product reflect your inner life?

Chapter 34: Total War, Totalitarianism, and the Arts

I. CHAPTER OBJECTIVE:

To examine the effects of total war and totalitarianism on the arts of the twentieth century

AM I FAMILIAR WITH:

- the historical significance and consequences of World Wars I and II?
- totalitarianism as exercised in Nazi Germany? in Russia? in China?
- specific examples of the impact of World Wars I and II on literature, the visual arts, music?
- the impact of totalitarianism on literature, painting, photography, music?

II. OUTLINE

A. Total War: World War I

    1. nature of the war

    2. literary responses

        a. poetry: Owen and Yeats

        b. prose: Remarque

        c. visual arts: Ernst, Grosz, and Leger

    3. experimental film

B. The Russian Revolution

    1. Lenin and Stalin

    2. socialist realism

C. The Great Depression

    1. literature

    2. mural painting

    3. photography

D. Totalitarianism and World War II

    1. Hitler and the Nazi order

    2. nature of the war

    3. poetry: Jarrell and Shuson

    4. prose: Heller and Wiesel

    5. film and photojournalism

E. The Arts in the War Era

    1. Picasso's *Guernica*

2. music

    a. Shostakovich and Prokofiev

    b. Britten

    c. Penderecki

F. Chinese Communism and the Arts

III. KEY TERMS: CAN I DEFINE/EXPLAIN

(What? Why important?)

total war

totalitarianism

Central/Allied forces

dulce et decorum est [dul SAY et day KOR um est]

"the second coming"

Great Depression

montage

vertical montage

mural

poster

Holocaust

documentary photography

gulag [GUL ahg]

Soviet

Axis powers

black humour

Catch-22

tone cluster

IV. KEY NAMES: CAN I IDENTIFY?

(Who? What? When? Where?)

Owen

Yeats [YAYTS]

Remarque [re MAHRK]

Ernst [ERNST]

Grosz [GROWS]

Leger [lay ZHAY]

Lenin

Stalin

Steinbeck

Benton

Rivera [ri VE ra]

Lange

Hitler

Jarrell

Shuson

Heller

Solzhenitsyn [sowl zhah NEET sin]

Wiesel [VEE zel]

Eisenstein [eye zen STINE]

Reifenstahl [REE fen shtal]

Miller

Guernica [GWER ni kah]

Shostakovich [shahs tah KOW vich]

Prokofiev

Copland

Britten

Penderecki [pen de RET skee]

Mao Zedong [mou tzay don]

V. KEY DATES

- 1911-1920 = Mexican Revolution
- 1911 = Chinese Revolution (overthrow of the Manchu)
- 1914-1918 = World War I
- 1917 = Russian Revolution
- 1926 = Stalin takes over Communist Russia
- 1936-1939 = Civil War in Spain
- 1939-1945 = World War II
- 1941 = Japan bombs Pearl Harbor
- 1945 = the United States bombs Hiroshima
- 1949 = Formation of the People's Republic of China

VI. VOCABULARY BUILDING

succinct

bootlegging

destitute

monochrome

threnody

VII. SAMPLE MULTIPLE CHOICE QUESTIONS

1. The combat weapon that devastates the soldiers in *All Quiet on the Western Front* is

    a. the atom bomb.

    b. the machine gun.

    c. poison gas.

    d. aerial bombing.

2. The leading political figure to emerge from the Russian Revolution of 1917 was

    a. Lenin.

    b. Stalin.

    c. Grosz.

    d. Hitler.

3. The literary style that dominated American fiction and the visual arts as a result of the Great Depression was

    a. surrealism.

    b. social realism.

    c. socialist realism.

    d. stream of consciousness.

4. The Holocaust was inspired by Hitler's theory of

    a. white supremacy.

    b. state control of the military.

    c. communism.

    d Aryan racial superiority.

5. NOT true of the era of total war and totalitarianism:

    a. photography and film provided lasting records of World War II

    b. black humour and nihilism characterized postwar literature

    c. the realities of the Holocaust went unrecorded in literature

    d. *Guernica* immortalized the aerial bombing of a civilian target

(Answers appear on page xi.)

VIII. VISUAL/SPATIAL EXERCISE

Map of Wartime Europe

On the map below, locate and identify the following places:

Warsaw	Brussels	Turkey	Poland
Gibraltar	London	Moscow	Switzerland
Bulgaria	Coventry	Munich	Berlin
Vichy	Prague	Greece	Serbia

IX. ESSAY QUESTIONS/WRITING EXERCISE

1. What specific images in the poems by Owen, Yeats, Jarrell, and Shuson best capture the rage and despair experienced during the wartime era?

2. Discuss the differences between "social realism" and "socialist realism" in the arts of the twentieth century. Cite examples wherever appropriate.

3. Select three works of art from this chapter that, in your view, convey most powerfully the violence and carnage of total war. How does each achieve its effect?

4. Critics hold that Aaron Copland wanted to create a language that would unite all Americans. Did he achieve this goal? How so? How might Copland's ambition reflect the wartime condition in which he composed?

5. FILMS FOR THIS CHAPTER: *Ballet méchanique; All Quiet on the Western Front; The Battleship Potemkin; From Here to Eternity; Catch-22.* See any one of these films and write a brief essay on how the film reflects the key ideas presented in this chapter.

X. MAKING CONNECTIONS

1. A TV logo reads: "Before TV, two world wars; after TV, none." In your view, has television affected our attitudes towards war? How so? Has film had the same kinds of effect? If so, how so?

2. Find a current billboard, photograph, or poster that clearly conveys a social message. Does the term "social realism" apply here? If so, how so?

3. Prior to taking this course, what personal experiences contributed to forming your knowledge of (or attitudes towards) modern warfare? How (if at all) has this chapter changed your perceptions of twentieth-century war?

4. How does warfare in the twenty-first century differ from that of the twentieth century?

Chapter 35: The Quest for Meaning

I. CHAPTER OBJECTIVE:

To examine the mood of alienation and anxiety as reflected in the arts at mid-century

AM I FAMILIAR WITH:

- the basic arguments of Sartrean existentialism?
- how each of the following reflects the quest for meaning at mid-century: existential literature; theater of the absurd; the poetry of Eliot and other poets at mid-century?
- the postwar cultural boom in America?
- the unique stylistic features of painting, architecture, music, and dance at mid-century?

II. OUTLINE

- A. The Historical Context
    - 1. the postwar condition
    - 2. utopias and dystopias
- B. Existentialism and Freedom
    - 1. Sartre and humanistic existentialism
    - 2. Christian existentialism
    - 3. existentialism and literature
    - 4. theater of the absurd: Beckett
- C. Film at Mid-Century
- D. The Quest for Meaning in Modern Poetry
    - 1. Eliot and Thomas
    - 2. Tagore
    - 3. Islamic poetry: Iqbal and Anwar
- E. The Visual Arts at Mid-Century
    - 1. painting
        - a. abstract expressionism
        - b. color field painting
        - c. regional realism
    - 2. sculpture
        - a. constructed sculpture
        - b. mobiles

3. architecture

    a. international style

    b. Saarinen

    c. Wright

F. Music and Dance at Mid-Century

    1. Cage and aleatory music

    2. Cunningham's radical choreography

III. KEY TERMS: CAN I DEFINE/EXPLAIN?

(What? Why important?)

utopia/dystopia

existentialism

bad faith

existential anguish

antihero

Islamic nationalism

the absurd

film noir [nwar]

femme fatale [fam fay TAL]

abstract expressionism

action painting

Zen

color field

unprimed canvas

constructed sculpture

mobile

international style

"less is more"

aleatory music [AY lee ah tor ee]

prepared piano

IV. KEY NAMES: CAN I IDENTIFY?

(Who? What? When? Where?)

Skinner

Huxley

Sartre [SAHRT]

Niebuhr [NEE ber]

Camus [kah MOO]

Miller

Malamud [MAL ah mud]

J. Alfred Prufrock

Thomas

Beckett

Tagore [tah GOOR]

Iqbal [IK bahl]

Anwar [AHN vahr]

Kurasawa [koo rah SAH wah]

Bergman

Kyokai [kee OH keye]

de Kooning

Kline

Pollock

Rothko

Frankenthaler

Hopper

Bacon

Segal

Smith

Calder

Mies van der Rohe [MEES VAN der row]

Seagram Building

Saarinen [SAHR en in]

Guggenheim Museum

Cage

I jing [ee CHEEN]

Cunningham

Black Mountain College

V. KEY DATES

- 1943 = Sartre publishes *Being and Nothingness*

- 1953 = Cage composes *4'33"*
- 1954 = Beckett publishes *Waiting for Godot*
- 1957-1959 = Wright's Guggenheim Museum constructed
- 1958 = First performance of Cunningham's *Summerspace*

VI. VOCABULARY BUILDING: CAN I DEFINE

essence

allegory

calligram

disavow

translucent

VII. SAMPLE MULTIPLE CHOICE QUESTIONS

1. Sartre held that each individual is

    a. born with an essential nature.

    b. determined by habits learned at childhood.

    c. the sum of his or her own actions.

    d. unable to choose between good and evil.

2. Christian existentialists focused upon

    a. whether or not God exists.

    b. the validity of Scripture.

    c. the need for ritual in religious life.

    d. the moral life of individuals.

3. Eliot's "Love Song of J. Alfred Prufrock"

    a. begins with lines from *Everyman*.

    b. is not a love song.

    c. identifies the hero as Hamlet.

    d. all of the above.

4. Cunningham's choreography was considered radical because it

    a. did not depend on music.

    b. excluded female dancers.

    c. required classical ballet shoes.

    d. employed polyrhythmic music.

5. NOT associated with the movement known as abstract expressionism:

   a. Kline

   b. de Kooning

   c. Hopper

   d. Pollock

(Answers appear on page xi.)

VIII. VISUAL/SPATIAL EXERCISE

In the GRAPHIC CLUSTER on the next page, write freely to explore associations between the styles and movements named in the "windows." You may write within or across the windows in the cluster.

THE QUEST FOR MEANING

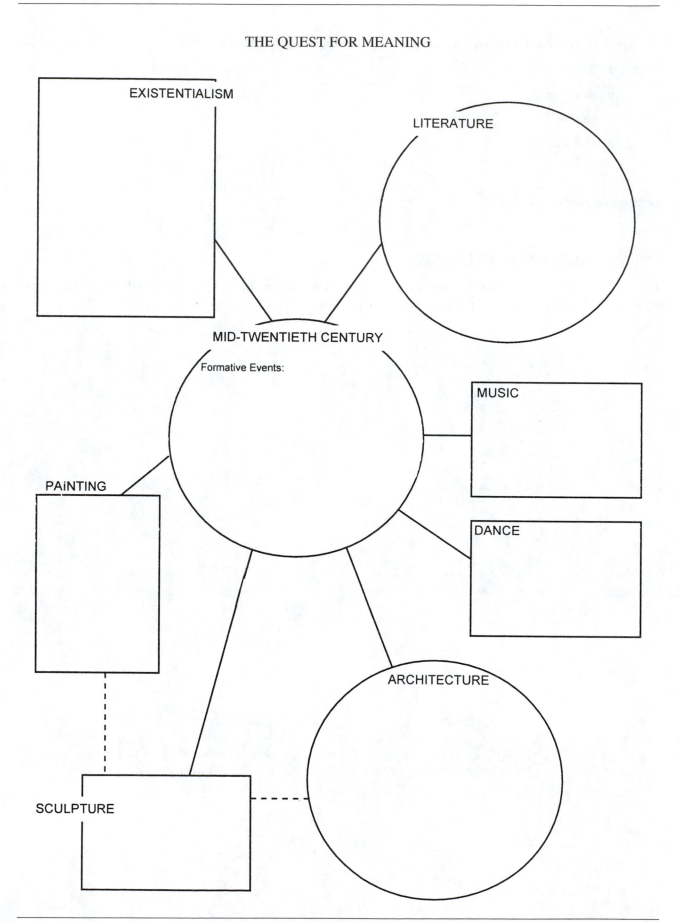

EXISTENTIALISM

LITERATURE

MID-TWENTIETH CENTURY

Formative Events:

MUSIC

PAiNTING

DANCE

ARCHITECTURE

SCULPTURE

IX. ESSAY QUESTIONS/WRITING EXERCISE

1. Explain each of the following: "existence precedes essence," "existential anguish," "bad faith." Can you find examples of each in the readings from this chapter?

2. Describe the personality of the antihero based on your reading of T.S. Eliot's "Prufrock". In what ways is this figure typically "modern"?

3. Hopper and other artists of this period were influenced by cinematic conventions, such as off center or "cropped" scenes. What other cinematic devices do you detect in Hopper's paintings? More generally, explore the relationship between film and the arts at mid-century.

4. Based on the excerpts in this chapter, discuss the ways in which the literature of the non-Western world differs from that of the West at mid-century. What sentiments in the poems on page 79 anticipate the current position of radical Islam?

5. FILMS FOR THIS CHAPTER: *Double Indemnity; Open City; Rashomon; Rear Window; The Seventh Seal.* See any one of these films and write an essay on how it reflects the key ideas and themes in this chapter.

X. MAKING CONNECTIONS

1. Drawing on your own personal history, describe an instance of "bad faith" in your (or some other person's) behavior and its consequences.

2. Choose a partner and enact the excerpt from Beckett's *Waiting for Godot* (Reading 6.12). How does it feel to be "in" either of these characters?

3. Visit a building (museum, bank, university center) that most closely resembles one by Saarinen, Wright, or Mies van der Rohe. How does the experience of being inside this modern structure differ from your experience inside more traditional buildings?

4. See the 2001 film on the life of Jackson Pollock. To what extent does it convey the unique role of the postwar abstract expressionists?

5. Compare the dramatic structure of Beckett's *Waiting for Godot* with any traditional play with which you are familiar.

XI. SYNTHESIS/ PART I: THE TRIUMPH OF MODERNISM

Write an extended essay on any ONE of the following:

1. What were the central factors and events that went into the shaping of modernism? To what extent did science and technology impact the arts of this period?

2. In your view, is it valid to claim that the arts of the early twentieth century reflect the "dehumanization" of art? Why or why not?

3. How does the early modern literature found in Chapters 31 to 35 differ from that which you have read in Chapters 27 to 30 of *The Humanistic Tradition?* Cite specific examples.

4. Write an essay that explains your own definitive view of "modernism." What is the most "modern" object in your room, study, or house? Why might you call it "modern"?

5. When your children look back on the early twentieth century, what might they value most? What might they scorn?

PART II. THE POSTMODERN TURN

Chapter 36: Identity and Liberation

I. CHAPTER OBJECTIVE:

To assess global movements for political, racial, and gender equality as reflected in the arts

AM I FAMILIAR WITH:

- the quest for liberation in colonial Latin America?
- the quest for racial equality and its proponents in the arts?
- African-American achievements in the visual arts? in music?
- the quest for gender equality as reflected in feminist literature and art?
- the role of ethnicity and ethnic identity in the arts?

II. OUTLINE

A. The Quest for Political Equality

    1. decolonization movements

    2. Neruda and Latin America

B. The Quest for Racial Equality

    1. Harlem Renaissance

       a. Hughes and Brooks

       b. Wright

    2. The Civil Rights Movement

       a. Martin Luther King

       b. Malcolm X

       c. Baldwin; Ellison; Alice Walker

    3. African-Americans and the visual arts

    4. African-Americans and jazz

    5. African-Americans and dance

C. The Quest for Gender Equality

    1. feminist protest: Woolf and de Beauvoir

    2. feminist poetry: Sexton, Sanchez, Rich

3. feminist art

    a. de Saint Phalle; Marisol; Mendieta

    b. Chicago's *Dinner Party*

    c. gender stereotypes: Sherman; Kruger; Neshat

4. sexual orientation and sexual freedom

D. Ethnicity and Identity

    1. ethnic literature: Cisneros

    2. ethnicity and the visual arts: Jiménez; Osorio

III. KEY TERMS: CAN I DEFINE/EXPLAIN?

(What? Why important?)

decolonization

Mahatma

Banana Republic

Harlem Renaissance

liberation

theology

Jim Crow

Civil Rights Act

black nationalism

apartheid [ah PAHR teyed]

Aunt Jemima

The Migration of the Negro

jazz

Jazz Age

ragtime

blues

swing

call and response

bebop

scat singing

cool jazz

steel band

hip-hop

feminism

misogyny [mis AH ge nee]

suffragette

Nana

Stonewall riots

AIDS

ethnicity

Latino/Latina

identity politics

Chicana [chee KA na]

IV. KEY NAMES: CAN I IDENTIFY?

(Who? What? When? Where?)

Ghandi

Neruda [ne ROO dah]

Hughes

Brooks

Richard Wright

Martin Luther King

Malcolm X

Fanon

Baldwin

Ellison

Walker

Lawrence

Saar

Colescott

Basquiat [BAS kee at]

Armstrong

Hardin

Bessie Smith

Gershwin

Ellington

Dunham

Primus

Spike Lee

Woolf

de Beauvoir [bow VWAHR]

Friedan [free DAN]

Sexton

Sanchez

Rich

de Saint-Phalle [de sayn FAL]

Marisol

Mendieta [men dee AY ta]

Chicago

Sherman

Kruger

Neshat

Mapplethorpe [MAY pul thowrp]

LeGuin [leh GWIN]

Kushner

Names Project Quilt

Cisneros [sees NER os]

Jiménez [hee MAY nays]

Osorio [o SO ree o]

V. KEY DATES

- 1920 = American women win the right to vote
- 1945 = Ellison begins *The Invisible Man*
- 1949 = de Beauvoir publishes *The Second Sex*
- 1952 = First contraceptive pills manufactured
- 1954 = U.S. Supreme Court bans school segregation
- 1963 = King jailed in Birmingham, Alabama; Friedan publishes *The Feminine Mystique*
- 1964 = King awarded the Nobel Peace Prize
- 1974-79 = Chicago directs *The Dinner Party*
- 1985 = AIDS Names Project Quilt is launched

VI. VOCABULARY BUILDING: CAN I DEFINE?

assimilate

colloquial

syncopate

androgyny

minstrel

pandemic

obsidian

VII. SAMPLE MULTIPLE CHOICE QUESTIONS

1. The theme of Neruda's poem, "The United Fruit Co.," is the

   a. positive effects of American economic policy in Latin America.

   b. need for Latin American social and religious reform.

   c. economic exploitation of Latin America by American corporations.

   d. rising tide of democracy in Latin American nations.

2. The poets Langston Hughes and Gwendolyn Brooks were writers of the

   a. Civil Rights Movement.

   b. Harlem Renaissance.

   c. Chicago Riots.

   d. Feminist Movement.

3. King's letter from a Birmingham jail asserts that

   a. violence in the name of equality is justified.

   b. any law that degrades human beings is unjust.

   c. blacks will always be strangers in the white world.

   d. the advertising media encourages racial discrimination.

4. In Walker's short story, *Elethia*, "Uncle Albert" is

   a. the owner of a restaurant.

   b. the benefactor of poor, local Blacks.

   c. a totally fictional character.

   d. the stereotypical equivalent of Aunt Jemima.

5. An important component of the music known as jazz:

   a. improvisation

   b. syncopation

   c. swing

   d. all of the above

6. The fastest growing population in the United States is

   a. African-American.

   b. Caucasian.

   c. Hispanic.

   d. Asian.

(Answers appear on page xi.)

VIII. ESSAY QUESTIONS/WRITING EXERCISE

1. Who were the central figures of the Harlem Renaissance, and what did they achieve?

2. Which examples of literature, art, and music in this chapter best reflect, in your view, the quest for racial equality? How so?

3. What reason does Simone de Beauvoir give for women's traditional subordination to men? Compare the point of view of either (a) Mary Wollstonecraft (Reading 4.20), (b) John Stuart Mill, (Reading 5.19), or (c) Virginia Woolf (Reading 6.24).

4. What feminist themes and motifs have preoccupied poets and painters in the last quarter of the twentieth century? Cite examples from literature and art.

5. FILMS FOR THIS CHAPTER: *Do the Right Thing; Malcolm X, Boyz in the Hood; Thelma and Louise; Boys in the Band.* See any one of these films and write a brief essay discussing how the film reflects the key ideas presented in this chapter.

IX. MAKING CONNECTIONS

1. Are there, in your view, any features of African-American art or music that are uniquely "black"? Are there, in your view, any features of women's art that are uniquely "female"?

2. How has your own ethnic and sexual identity influenced your approach to the humanities?

3. Attend a live jazz performance. What aspects of this experience differ from those of attending a rock concert, symphony concert, or the like?

4. Why is rage a frequent feature or characteristic of art that deals with issues of race, gender, and sexual identity?

Chapter 37: The Information Age: Message and Meaning

I. CHAPTER OBJECTIVE:

To examine contemporary literature as it reflects the impact of mass media and information technology

AM I FAMILIAR WITH:

- the ways in which high technology and the information explosion have influenced late twentieth and early twenty-first-century culture?
- the ways in which new directions in science and philosophy have influenced Information Age culture?
- the basic features of postmodern literature? magic realism? the literature of social conscience? science fiction?

II. OUTLINE

   A. Historical Context

      1. developments in information technology

         a. television

         b. computers

      2. the birth of space exploration

      3. new directions in science and philosophy

         a. string theory

         b. chaos theory

         c. mapping the human genome

         d. language theory

   B. Postmodernism

   C. Literature in the Information Age

      1. postmodern poetry: Paz, Ashbery, and Walcott

      2. magic realism: Allende

      3. the literature of social conscience

         a. poetry: Snyder and Szymborska

         b. prose: Achebe and Oates

      4. science fiction and film

III. KEY TERMS: CAN I DEFINE/EXPLAIN?

(What? Why important?)

global paradigm

computopia

string theory

genome

chaos theory

deconstruction

postmodernism

magic realism

multiculturalism

sutra [SOO trah]

science fiction

IV. KEY NAMES: CAN I IDENTIFY?

(Who? What? When? Where?)

Kundera [kun DEH ra]

Ellul [el LUL]

Greene

Pert

Chopra

Wittgenstein [VIT gen shteyen]

Foucault [foo KOW]

Rorty

Paz [PAHZ]

Ashbery

Walcott

Allende [eye YEN day]

Snyder

Szymborska [sheem BOR skah]

Achebe [ah CHAY bay]

Oates

Clarke

Kubrick

2001: A Space Odyssey

V. KEY DATES

- 1933 = Electronic television developed
- 1951 = Color TV introduced in the U.S.

- 1953 = First commercially successful computer
- 1957 = Russia launches first artificial earth satellite
- 1964-1973 = Vietnam War
- 1969 = First lunar landing
- 1991 = Collapse of Soviet Communism
- 1995 = Hubble Space Telescope launched
- 2000 = Mapping of the human genome

VI. VOCABULARY BUILDING: CAN I DEFINE?

robotics

paradigm

commodity

permutation

millennium

VII. SAMPLE MULTIPLE CHOICE QUESTIONS

1. The postmodern concern with language is most evident in the poetry of

    a. Eliot and Yeats.

    b. Oates and Walcott.

    c. Snyder and Achebe.

    d. Paz and Ashbery.

2. Kubrick's *2001 A Space Odyssey* was based on

    a. an actual event.

    b. a medieval legend.

    c. a short story.

    d. none of the above.

3. The effort to achieve a "theory of everything" is configured in

    a. Chaos theory.

    b. String theory.

    c. Deconstruction.

    d. Language theory.

4. The term "postmodern" was first introduced in association with

    a. architecture.

    b. music.

    c. sculpture.

    d. painting.

5. Snyder's "Smokey the Bear Sutra" expresses his concern with potential

    a. global war.

    b. computer-style dehumanization.

    c. ecological disaster.

    d. all of the above.

6. A major theme in Achebe's story, *Dead Men's Path,* is

    a. African disunity.

    b. age versus youth.

    c. religion versus science.

    d. tradition versus innovation.

(Answers appear on page xi.)

VIII. ESSAY QUESTIONS/WRITING EXERCISE

1. Discuss the ways in which the readings in this chapter reflect a concern for language and communication. Does the medium in any of these readings seem to overtake the message? If so, how so?

2. In what ways is the "global paradigm"—the interrelatedness of all parts of the planet—reflected in the readings in this chapter?

3. In your view, which of the readings in this chapter best reflects or defines the culture of your own time and place? How so?

4. Evaluate the role of television and film on Information Age culture. Cite specific examples, such as the way in which TV violence parallels fictional stories such as that by Oates.

5. FILMS FOR THIS CHAPTER: *2001: A Space Odyssey; 1984; Star Wars; Dune; Terminator 2*. See any one of these films and write a brief essay discussing how the film reflects the key ideas presented in this chapter.

IX. MAKING CONNECTIONS

1. Write a short story in one of the literary styles discussed in this chapter: magic realism, social conscience, science fiction.

2. In 1997, the Russian chess master Garry Kasparov lost a match with an IBM computer. What are the implications of the IBM victory? Can you offer other examples of "Man versus Machine" in today's world?

3. Describe what you would identify as a typically "postmodern experience" (either real or fictional). How does it differ from a "modern" experience?

4. Read a recent science fiction work, then one written twenty years ago. How do they differ? What do these differences reflect about our rapidly changing world?

5. Find and discuss examples in the arts on the subject of terrorism. Are any as effective as Szymborska's poem, "The Terrorist, He Watches" (page 136)?

Chapter 38: Image and Sound in the Information Age

I. CHAPTER OBJECTIVE:

To examine the visual arts, music, and dance of the late twentieth and early twenty-first centuries as they reflect the impact of mass media and information technology

AM I FAMILIAR WITH:

- the wide variety of postmodern styles: pop art, assemblage, minimalism, conceptual art, total art, neorealism, neoexpressionism, social conscience art?
- the shaping role of high-tech media (acrylic, fiberglass, aluminum, etc.) on the arts?
- the basic features of postmodern architecture, opera, and dance?
- the revolutionary effects of electronics on music and musical composition?
- the impact of the computer on the arts?
- the dominance of globalism in the contemporary arts?

II. OUTLINE

  A. The Visual Arts

    1. pop art

      a. Warhol

      b. Johns; Oldenberg; Lichtenstein

    2. assemblage

      a. Rauschenberg

      b. Chamberlain; Nevelson

    3. geometric abstraction, op, minimalism, neon, kinetic

      a. Judd; Noguchi

      b. Riley; Stella

      c. Chryssa

    4. new realism

      a. Estes; Close

      b. Hanson

    5. new expressionism

      a. Kiefer

    6. social conscience

      a. Kienholz; Azaceta

      b. Abakanowicz

      c. Wang Guangyi

7. total art

   a. performance art; happenings

   b. environmental art: Smithson; the Christos

8. video art

   a. Paik

   b. Viola

B. Computers and the Visual Arts

   1. impact of digital imaging

      a. Yasumasa Morimura

      b. Mariko Mori

C. Contemporary Film

   1. experimental film

   2. art film

   3. computers and film

D. The Visual Arts and the Global Paradigm

E. Architecture in the Information Age

   1. Moore; Pei

   2. Gehry

F. Music in the Information Age

   1. microtonality: Ligeti

   2. minimalism: Glass

   3. postmodern opera: Corigliano

   4. electronic music: Babbitt; McLean

   5. rock and its spin-offs

G. Music and the Global Paradigm

   1. reggae; multicultural pastiche

   2. free jazz/new jazz: Roberts; Marsalis

H. Dance in the Information Age

III. KEY TERMS: CAN I DEFINE/EXPLAIN?

(What? Why important?)

pop art

silkscreen

assemblage

geometric abstraction

op art

minimalism

kinetic art

total art

happenings

conceptual art

performance art

environmental art

earth sculpture

new realism (neorealism)

new expressionism (neoexpressionism)

social conscience art

digital imaging

virtual reality

cynical realism

deconstructivism

geodesic

microtonality

musique concrète

synthesizer

rock

reggae [reh GAY]

new jazz

butoh [boo tow]

IV. KEY NAMES: CAN I IDENTIFY?

(Who? What? When? Where?)

Warhol

Johns

Oldenburg

Lichtenstein

Rauschenberg [ROU shen berg]

Chamberlain

Nevelson

Stella

Riley

Judd

Noguchi [now GOO chee]

Chryssa

Holzer

Klein

Kaprow

Christo [KRIS tow]

Smithson

Estes

Close

Hanson

Kiefer

Kienholz [KEYEN holtz]

Azaceta [ah zah CHAY tah]

Abakanowicz [ah bah KAHN oh vitz]

Paik [PAYK]

Viola

Yasumasa Morimura [mor ee MOR a]

Mariko Mori

Wang Guangyi [wan gan ZEE]

Yanagi

World Flag Ant Farm

Zang Yimou [shan zee MOO]

Piazza d'ltalia [pee AHZ ah di TAHL yah]

Pei [PAY]

Gehry

Ligeti

Stockhausen

Glass

Corigliano [kor ee LYAN oh]

McLean

the Beatles

Marley

Marsalis

V. KEY DATES

- 1976 = Glass composes *Einstein on the Beach*
- 1988 = Pei designs the Louvre Pyramid
- 1992 = Corigliano composes *Ghosts of Versailles*
- 2000 = Gehry completes the Guggenheim Museum at Bilbao

VI. VOCABULARY BUILDING: CAN I DEFINE?

ominous

hypermedia

oscillate

quintessential

digital

virtual

bioengineering

barrage

acoustics

VII. SAMPLE MULTIPLE CHOICE QUESTIONS

1. One of the principal influences on the rise of pop art was

   a. mass advertising.

   b. language theory.

   c. computers.

   d. digital imaging.

2. NOT associated with the development of electronic music:

   a. Stockhausen

   b. Babbitt

   c. Glass

   d. McLean

3. Minimalism, op art, and geometric abstraction have this in common: they

   a. are all forms of pop art.

   b. are largely nonobjective.

   c. employ assembled parts.

   d. depend on electronic power.

4. The pioneer figure in the use of computers and the visual arts is

    a. Rauschenberg.

    b. Warhol.

    c. Paik.

    d. Kiefer.

5. Which of the following do not belong together:

    a. Happenings/performance art

    b. Environmental art/earth sculpture

    c. Minimalism/op art

    d. Geometric abstraction/Social conscience art

6. NOT characteristic of the end of the twentieth century in the arts:

    a. the blurring of the lines between various artforms

    b. the appropriation of non-Western themes and styles

    c. the emergence of a single, clearly definable style in the visual arts

    d. the practice of writing operas based on literary works

(Answers appear on page xi.)

VIII. ESSAY QUESTIONS/WRITING EXERCISE

1. Which of the art styles in this chapter might be considered "serious"? Which are "humorous"? How so? Why are humor and parody so important to postmodern expression?

2. Select examples from advertisements in current magazines that reflect the influence of pop art; of minimalism; of geometric abstraction. How has the world of advertising come to depend on "high" art?

3. A critic wrote that once John Cage composed *4' 33"* there was nowhere to go but sideways. Using this novel statement as a starting point, discuss the unique features of classical music since 1953.

4. Assess the influence of electronic technology on contemporary art or music.

5. FILMS FOR THIS CHAPTER: *Nashville; Schindler's List; Raise the Red Lantern; Forrest Gump; Last Judgment.* See any one of these films and write a brief essay discussing how the film reflects the key ideas in this chapter.

IX. MAKING CONNECTIONS

1. In your opinion, which artworks discussed in this chapter might become part of "the canon"? Which might your children's children be studying in their humanities courses thirty years from today? Why so?

2. Find current examples of social conscience art, literature, and music. Is "rap music" a form of social conscience art? Why or why not?

3. Speculate on how current forms of computer entertainment (video games, the Internet, and the like) might affect the future of the arts.

4. Concerning the East and West, a nineteenth-century poet once claimed that "never the twain shall meet." Do you agree with this point of view? Why or why not?

X. SYNTHESIS/ PART II: THE POSTMODERN TURN

Write an extended essay on any ONE of the following:

1. Discuss the differences between modernism (the style that dominated the arts until approximately mid-century) and postmodernism, or the arts of the late twentieth century. Cite specific examples to make your case.

2. Consider the role of the female artist in the late twentieth century. What differences can you detect between nineteenth-century female artists and those of the present?

3. Isolate the unique features in art, music, or dance of the last twenty-five years. How do these differ from the main features of the art or music of the previous fifty years?

4. At the end of the nineteenth century, art for art's sake was a dominant movement. At the beginning of the twentieth century, abstraction was the rage. Why has the art of the last twenty years come to embrace so much social conscience expression? Cite specific examples.

5. Film is often called the "quintessential medium of the modern era." Would you agree with this assessment? Cite specific examples to defend or refute.